Generative:
Adj. 1. having the
power of producing
or originating
2. to bring to life

THE GENERATIVE ORGANIZATION

Reactive Behavior to Inspired Performance

A CEO's Transformational Journey
To Change the Game & Generate Inspired Performance

By
William J. Schwarz

For permissions requests, contact the publisher at:
Aardvark Global Publishing Company
9587 S. Grandview Drive
Salt Lake City, Utah 84092

Or the author at:
The CEO Alliance
1641 Doncaster Dr.
Atlanta, GA 30309
Phone: 404-875-4180
Fax: 404-875-4452
bill@theceoalliance.com
www.inspiredperformance.org

Printed in the United States
10 9 8 7 6 5 4 3 2 1
ISBN 1-59971-647-X

Cover Design by Elaine Hightower
Cover Illustration by Ursula Stroebel
Printed by Service Technologies

At Senco Products, we were an old line organization, doing things in a traditional manner. We brought in Bill Schwarz and actually had the opportunity to live the experiences that Mitchell Crandall goes through in this exciting tale. The processes described herein can actually transform not only you as a leader, but the entire organization. It brings a company alive, releases its energy and aligns its people to accomplish real, lasting, sustainable change. It did so for us. Bill has captured the essence of what it takes to lead an organization to greatness. He gives the secret formula for an executive to become an organizational architect and designer. He has given us the strategies for controlling our organizational destiny.

Norm Day
CEO/Chairman of the Board
SenCorp

Good to Great is an illuminating historical research study of companies. It is a great book. *The Generative Organization, From Reactive Behavior to Inspired Performance* is the how to manual to achieve that greatness. It challenges the leader who has faced great peril and crises in growing his/her business to come face to face with their own accountability and responsibility for the future of their organization. I have never read a business book that so captivated me. This is written in such a manner that you learn as you go and experience it as if you were there. It will change your entire view of business and leadership. It did mine.

Jerry Scher
PRISCO

By weaving specific tools into a compelling parable, Bill Schwarz teaches us how to manage, lead — and live — better. Dale Carnegie meets Zen, and we the readers are much better off. I recommend it highly.

Strauss Zelnick
CEO of Zelnick Media
Chariman of Take Two Interactive & Time Life

When we first began to apply the priciples that are revealed in this book we were in the bottom quartile of our industry. Within two years we were in the top 10% of our industry and have maintained that status in all six of the growth strategies Bill Schwarz reveals in the story about Mitchell Crandall. This had occurred while going through industry consolidations, rollups, new aggressive low cost (knock-off) competitors and dealers who were caught up in very costly bankruptcies. Yet we innovated, executed strategically, changed the entire way in which we approached our business all based on the principles outlined in Bill Schwarz's book. We know this story well. We lived it. There is not one thing in this book that we have not seen work within our organization. It took hard work and required change in thinking. Not an easy task. The stories we have to tell are also about how lives were changed (from warehousemen to myself). They are just as vital as how we have increased margins, grown market share, added new product lines and formed entirely new organizations.

Read this book — if you have the courage to implement your growth strategy — from the inside out.

Bud Mingledorff, CEO
Mingledorff's

If you are leading an organization, this book is like a guidance system that tells you where to turn and warns you before you make the wrong decisions. There is a lot of talk about working on the organization, not it. This book tells you how. The principles you will find here have profoundly impacted the direction our company is headed and have personally changed my life. Our firm has never been as focused and as energized as we have been since we started working together with Bill Schwarz to create our future and build a Generative Organization. We set a sales record last year and are on our way to setting another one this year.

As a former college professor and now businessman and consultant, I must tell you not to read this book unless you want to change. If you do, then don't just read it, study it before every major decision you make.

Edwin T. Cornelius, Ph.D.,
Founder and president,
Cornelius & Associates

I was fortunate enough (though somewhat painfully) to go through the process that Mitchell Crandall experienced in this book. When I made it to the other side, I had learned a complete new set of skills — the skills that it takes to be a change agent.

I first encountered and engaged Bill Schwarz and applied the principles outlined in this must-read book as the founder and CEO of Digital Communications Associates (DCA). It resulted in us working our way out of a totally reinforcing vicious circle of reactive behavior. Then we merged with another out-of-control company and had to do it again. As we continued to grow, we had to learn how to manage change in the middle of a perfect storm. We did it and became the darling of the hi-tech world in the Southeast. We continued to grow the company and were able to very successfully go public. The shareholders (many of whom were employees) experienced great returns on their investment and trust.

The change produced by this process frees the enthusiasm and creative energies of everyone in a manner that propels a company to new levels of innovation and inspired performance.

Getting there is a rough ride, but the results are truly astounding when accomplished.

John Alderman
Founder and Chairman
Digital Communications Associates

I n *The Generative Organization,* Bill Schwarz, in the tradition of the enlightened masters, tells a story that transforms the reader's point of view. Through anecdote and parable, Bill weaves the principles of enlightened leadership in a manner that moved me to a new level of understanding of organizational cause and effect. Business leaders need to study this text in great detail. It's going to change the way we do business in America. Within this text are the secret answers to why we never achieved a 30-hour work week, and why some of the best companies still can't make money for their investors.

Michael G. Beason
Chairman, Supplier Excellence Alliance

When we first began applying *The Generative Organization* principles and practices mapped out in this fascinating book, I had my doubts. I knew we needed to bring about change, yet we had tried just about every new idea the industry leaders suggested. We poured money and resources into keeping up with the rapidly changing credit union and financial marketplace — and it was killing us — but we didn't know it. Within a few weeks after mapping out our underlying structure (just as Mitchell Crandall did) and discovering our leverage points, we aligned everyone around them and executed with a truly inspired organization's buy in. We formed a design team and change coalitions to implement all of our growth strategies. We have not looked back. The results have been spectacular.

This book captures our entire experience, except for the 'sweat lodge.' It is a must read for all executives who are serious about understanding their organization, themselves and in building a team that can execute strategically.

Kent Herbert
CEO, Eastern Florida Financial
Credit Union

Bill Schwarz's book, *The Generative Organization*, is a must read for any progressive leader. It is one that I personally could not put down once I started to read it. Bill is a wonderful story teller, and one with a message of how to succeed in today's complex world. His stories are well crafted and one after another cut through the complexity to a simple message. He takes the reader on a journey we all must take at some level if we are going to make a difference. It is based on the natural way the world works . . . Systems Thinking . . . as living systems exist all around us and are the way we need to THINK DIFFERENTLY in all that we do. Everything is interconnected in today's global economy and this book absolutely hits the executive reader over the head with a 2x4. Don't even think about growing your business without the knowledge and wisdom in this book. It cuts to the core as to why companies fail to execute strategically.

If there is one book you read this year, this is it.

Stephen Haines
Founder and CEO, The Centre
for Strategic Management

This book is incredible. It reads like a guided missile that strikes right at the heart of our industry. Whether a company is in survival or growing rapidly, Bill Schwarz has written the manual for taking an organization out of reactive behavior and to the next level of greatness. His message fits for small business as much as the very largest and most sophisticated. It guides the CEO down a path of self-discovery that leads to being able to assess, design, align and execute growth strategies and achieve competitive advantage.

Rachel Ann Shattah
President / CEO
Printing Industry Association of Georgia, Inc.

I have written 20 books on quality and management, traveled the world addressing executives; after reading *The Generative Organization*, I have finally found the wisdom that CEOs need to have in order to implement quality and major improvements into their organization. Bill Schwarz presents real down-to-earth (the Law of Nature) principles and practices for leading an organization. He says, "You can only control what has not yet happened" and then tells you how.

Most executives look in the rear view mirror (at financials and what happened yesterday). Bill gives us the ability to create the future. He takes the theory of systems thinking and makes it real, usable and empowering. This book takes each reader on a vision quest that results in them seeing the world through another set of eyes.

Great reading; a real page turner that you can not put down if you are leading your organization through change and strategic growth.

H. James Harrington, PH. D
Chairman of Harrington Institute
Past Chair of International Academy of Quality

I read Bill's book three times, and after six months of implementing his concepts I was able to reduce my inventory by 50%, increase my annualized inventory run from 4 to 9 times, and increase my gross margins by 6 points.

Kevin Melendy, President
Spectral Response
Member, The Brain Trust

Acknowledgements

I wish to express my heartfelt thanks to the two most precious women in my life, my wife, Lauren Black Schwarz and my daughter, Vail Davidson. Without their astute editorial skills this would not be the book that it is today. They worked tirelessly over each word and phrase, taking feedback from CEOs who read the drafts and incorporated their insights and suggestions. They are precious and I love them deeply. Without them and my son, Kord, I would not have known love.

A special acknowledgement must be made to Harvey LaReau who has kept the development process alive in building our navigational guidance system for the Center for Inspired Performance. Thanks Harvey. Thanks also to Elaine Hightower of Trio Media Group for her design direction and creative input.

Without a doubt this book is written on the shoulders of giants who have led the way in organizational transformation, systems dynamics and thinking and organizational leadership. But the real source of validation of all the principles and practices laid out here are those individuals and companies who have truly risked, trusted, become vulnerable, stepped out on their own, put a stake in the ground, lived by giving and keeping their word. These courageous individuals are everywhere you look when change is based on fundamental truths, governing principles and the willingness to step out and execute strategically.

I personally have had the opportunity to work closely with some of the greatest minds of our times while running an honors program during my undergraduate years in college. These included Arnold Toynbee,

Ayn Rand, Eric Hoffer, Bertrand Russell, Mortimer Adler, Eric Fromm and Victor Frankl.

Later, when establishing our Executive MBA and the Corporate Satellite Television Network I worked closely with George Odiorne, Fred Herzberg, Ken Blanchard, Edward Deming, Phillip Crosby, M. Scot Myers, Larry Miller, David Merrill, Stephen Covey, Chris Argyrus, Ed Schien, Warren Bennis, Jim Golembievski, Larry Wilson, James Harrington and have been influenced the the work of Jay Forrester and Willard Fey (my systems dynamics mentor), Peter Senge and the founders of systems thinking. In understanding and applying individual assessments I want to acknowledge the breakthrough thinking and research of Dan Harrison, Ph.D., developer of the Harrison Assessments (referenced in this book).

Thanks to all of you.

Bill

TABLE OF CONTENTS

FOREWORD

When The CMD Group (The Construction Market Data Group) first engaged Bill Schwarz and The CEO Alliance to work with us we did a thorough check of the clients he had done work for over the past decade. They all had the same thing to say. Do not take this on unless you are ready for real change. Change at the core of your organization. It will change what you focus on and what you do — completely. They said it would take courage to examine the cause and consequences of reactive behavior, and that it would be difficult to let go of it or give it up. I personally found that even though our reactive behavior was destructive, counterproductive and sucking resources down a bottomless pit, it was also addictive. Reactive behavior was exciting and full of surprises.

Given my competitive nature, the more they made it sound tough, the more I liked it. But even though I liked what I heard, I had no idea what I was actually getting into. Now as I read this book, it is like it was written about us, indeed myself, and almost every successful CEO I know.

We had done it all "right" — we thought. We were capturing market share and had made very strategic acquisitions and were growing the business globally. We were right in the middle of the dot-com bubble (no one knew it was a bubble, as we all talked about the new and old economy) and had several of the biggest players waving huge stock offers in front of us. I felt I was a visionary CEO in our marketplace and was leading our company into the clear blue sky. I thought we had just grown too fast and therefore needed a little tweaking — just needed to clarify our vision, mission and values and get buy-in, that kind of thing. Boy was I wrong.

Prior to working with Bill, we had brought several of the top consulting firms in to look at us. They did all the number crunching, interviewed everyone, ran surveys, mapped processes, studied the marketplace and made recommendations based on their way of viewing the global world we were playing in. They said the solution to our problems resided in changing our IT infrastructure. This led to a major software installation and their consultants working with us to design and implement it. From there we experienced a tragedy/comedy of the greatest proportions and an endless process of change orders and add-ons. I became close friends with the high profile software house CEO and even built strategic alliances with him to offset the cost. Unbeknownst to us or them, their project had already crashed and burned while we were thought it was going great. We were not able to see it until we began the process outlined in this book. We were just digging our way out of the hole we were in, only using technology to do it faster.

As I read and re-read each chapter of this book it brought back all of the memories of what it took for us to go from reactive behavior to inspired performance. We had to address our way of thinking about everything. That included who we thought we were as leaders and executives, what business we were actually in, what we had to do to position ourselves competitively and how to execute our growth strategy. It was humbling to go through, but it paid off in huge dividends for our investors, shareholders and indeed myself.

If you are interested, here is what we encountered that really parallels everything you are about to experience as you read this book.

First, we discovered we spent close to 85 percent of our time in a reactive state (even though we believed we were being strategic in all our decisions.) We were opening new branches, adding more complex and innovative products and services and servicing more sophisticated high leverage accounts with greater margins. This stretched our resources, causing us to take short cuts everywhere we looked, including our selection, development and promotion of people. We were on a sprint to beat our competitors into the internet market and dominate the digital world of construction market data while maintaining all of our existing (brick and mortar) publications. Exciting time! Of course it was, but little did we know that we were throwing fuel on the fires we thought we were putting out — all the while actually limiting our growth — not growing our business.

Second, we worked late into the evening for several days with Bill's help and mapped the patterns and underlying structure that was causing our reactive behavior. We discovered our company was "working perfectly, just like it was designed." When we were able to see the cause (the principles we were violating) we also saw the leverage points that would completely remove the source of our reactive behavior. From then on we simply aligned everyone around those leverage points and eliminated the reactive behavior that had been consuming us.

Third, we formed a design team and several change coalitions to remove our limits to growth and become a focus-driven company. Then we began the process of developing core competencies. Ultimately, we focused our attention on becoming a competency development company. That is what gave us our competitive advantage.

We sold the business and became a part of one of the largest business information corporations in the world. The pay day for us was substantial. Some of my sadness was that we did not take the company to the next levels of performance that we had positioned ourselves to achieve as a Generative Organization — before we sold it (for all cash).

Arol Wolford
Former Chairman and CEO
The CMD Group

INTRODUCTION

C EO's face great difficulties. These difficulties are complex, long-term, deeply rooted and systemic. Some are known and well understood. Most are hidden, undiscovered and invisible to the untrained eye. Difficulties which are visible are seen as problems, surprises, unexpected events, crises (or even opportunities). They get our attention. They are visible because they cause damage or produce unwanted effects. Based on what the CEO sees, decisions are made and actions are taken. The side effects of these decisions and actions result in further problem solving and additional difficulties. This is a revolving door that produces a centripetal force and becomes self-reinforcing.

Herein lies an even greater difficulty for the leader. Most leaders, executives or managers think they have clarified what the situation is, defined and solved the problem. The belief is that an intelligent, informed decision has been made that will make things better, or at least prevent them from getting worse.

The real problem, however, is this: *The actual cause of the difficulty is seldom known.* Cause is not in the same time or space as the effect (or problem). Cause, by its very nature, is invisible; it cannot be seen. Cause is rooted in the violation of or adherence to specific governing principles and laws. This violation or adherence is rooted in the values and beliefs of an organization's leadership.

Therefore, the 'corrective actions' taken rarely address cause. Sadly, they do not solve even the visible effects of real cause. Therefore, these (un) solved problems come back over and over, needing to be re-solved time and again. Without knowledge of the underlying cause, most actions will even reinforce and strengthen core weaknesses. When this occurs, the original cause of the weaknesses is made more powerful.

More often than not, this kind of problem solving creates a situation in which *yesterday's solutions become today's problems.* Well-intentioned leaders who fix things and solve problems in this fashion end up being a detriment to their organization, because they operate out of a fundamentally flawed thinking process. Such incorrect thinking is based on false judgments about people, processes, programs, projects, money, profits, and losses. Even perceived positive results are often laden with serious detrimental side effects. These side effects are often worse than the original upset or problem, yet these solutions often become policy.

When problems keep recurring and people are caught in their vicious grip, the corporate vision statement is rarely seen as real. To be real, a vision statement needs to be based on specific leverage points that are causal in nature. It needs to guide the direction of every person in the organization and do so by taking into account the systemic nature of what it takes to grow the organization.

True leadership is not possible when decisions are based on false data, misperception or incorrect beliefs. It is only possible based on fundamental truths or principles, accurate data and a well-grounded philosophy of causality. From these guideposts you can see inward, expand outward, upward and then forward.

Leadership capable of controlling an organization's destiny needs to be based on a philosophy of causality that is determined by:

- knowing the way the world works
- knowing how organizations work
- understanding the nature of man and man's human nature
- working with the laws of nature
- adhering to governing principles

When the principles that determine individual and organizational behavior are adhered to, people in teams become centers of learning and growth. They become capable of inspired performance.

These same principles provide the foundation that allows a leader to think like an organizational architect and designer. When leaders apply design principles they become wise stewards of shareholder value. They and their teams can maximize the use of all of their resources to achieve results.

Working with design principles results in the ability to create the future. Creating the future requires freedom from the illusions of the problems, crises and pressures that trap you in a vicious circle. It gives you leverage. Leverage is accomplished by focusing your attention on and applying the right amount of pressure to a specific point that causes a balanced state of growth. It eliminates the source of upset conditions and removes limits to growth.

The purpose of this book is for you to be able to study the principles and tools that allow you to use your highest leverage effectively. Using leverage enlightens and empowers in a sustainable manner. It develops core competencies that attain a competitive advantage by achieving sustained inspired performance. Core competencies determine the success or failure of most leadership action.

When the conscious development of core competencies and the application of governing principles are combined they form a navigational guidance system. They become the basis for attaining sustained, inspired performance and an optimum rate of growth.

Join Mitchell Crandall as he discovers the sources of his reactive behavior, the laws of nature, the design principles and navigational guidance system that allows him to ultimately build a Generative Organization and achieve inspired performance.

CHAPTER 1 *The Dilemma*

Mitchell Crandall sat for what seemed like an eternity. His head was spinning. He felt totally disoriented. The anxiety he had experienced the past several mornings was now consuming him. It felt like a twenty-pound weight was on his chest and he could barely breathe. His world had just come crumbling down around him.

Was this how it would end? After achieving eight years of steady growth, never missing any projections and having everything in place to go public, it all seemed to be coming apart. His energy was depleted. He just could not hold things together anymore. "We did it all. There was no stone unturned. We built this company right," he reassured himself, knowing deep inside that something critical was missing. He had never been able to put his finger on it.

In the midst of his anxiety anger seeped in. "Where were his bankers? When they wanted his business they promised the moon. Where were his board and investor group when he really needed them for the first time?" He had handpicked all of them.

AFTER ACHIEVING EIGHT YEARS OF STEADY GROWTH, NEVER MISSING ANY PROJECTIONS AND HAVING EVERYTHING IN PLACE TO GO PUBLIC, IT ALL SEEMED TO BE COMING APART.

Mitch had always considered his venture capital group his sure thing — his trump card in a short-term cash crunch. Now they had pulled the plug on him. By over-extending on several of their investments they had depleted what he considered his cash-reserve fund. He stood to lose everything. Not just a major client, but also his company.

The most painful part was that it was his close friend, David, who had served under him in Vietnam and now ran the venture capital group who had let him down. Mitch had initially formed the VC group to fund the company, and brought David in to run it. Now they were in their own financial crisis and were teetering on the verge of being acquired or selling off assets. This could shift the control of the board to his bankers and a new group that he did not know. When he asked David who the new group was, he replied, rather coolly, that they could not disclose the 'other party.' When Mitch demanded full disclosure, David said he would have to contact their attorneys in the morning. He gave Mitch their phone number and hung up. Mitch felt total betrayal. It was like a dagger through his heart. It felt like David had reached into his chest and yanked his heart right out of his body. His lifeblood seemed to be drained from him. This was the final blow.

"It will take a miracle to save the company now," he said to himself, "a miracle," his mind sorting through his dilemma in a sort of jumble. Again, for what seemed like an endless number of times, he pulled out his yellow pad to go over his situation. He had to get back into control. It was imperative that no one could sense the state he was in. The control he had so carefully orchestrated was suddenly gone. What had happened? What was he missing? What was the solution? It had to be there. He just needed to back away and look at it differently — think outside of the box, as he had often encouraged his management team to do.

The Building Crisis

SINCE 9/11, TWO OF HIS SUPPLIERS HAD SHUT DOWN. "Nothing I can do about that," he said to himself. Then another supplier informed him they were cutting him off. Their credit policies on anyone over 30 days had changed. That left him unable to fill orders that were already behind in production and due to be shipped on Friday. He had already furloughed 15 percent of his workforce and permanently laid off five percent. Right now, it would take all of them to get these orders out the door. He had cut deep into the fiber of the organization to stay alive. Instinctively, Mitch knew he had severely damaged it.

The cause of the cash crunch was simple, and certainly not his fault. He simply had not received payment on two of his largest orders from last month. Despite making major concessions to the client, they had not kept their word on the payment terms. Although the bank Mitch had done business with for years was sympathetic, they had been recently acquired and merged into one of the large national banks. Now their only focus was to run things based on financial formulas. This time they wanted personal guarantees.

Mitch continued to reflect on how he had been the industry leader in implementing all of the latest technologies and business process improvements. He had invested heavily in new software, and now that it was finally at about 89 percent, his IT director (the only person who really understood the system) had left and joined the company that sold him the software.

Despite his focus on identifying endless ways to lower costs, improve productivity and quality, people on the front line never really bought in. A lot of the strategies and processes did not get fully implemented. Yet there was always a direct payback.

"Even though we went through all of the ISO certification processes," Mitch contemplated, "little real change came out of it to benefit the company. I guess it was critical we do it for our global marketing strategy — though it added layers of documentation. Boy, something's been lost in all of this.

"I remember when we were young and growing," he continued reflecting. "We seemed to have a different spirit. We were like a big family and everyone wanted to contribute and give their best. None of these programs have been able to create that spirit again. Somehow, we need to get back to our roots. We need to find what is missing — recapture what we seem to have lost."

"I wonder what happened?" he pondered sadly.

"Well, I can't dwell on these things," he thought, shaking himself from his reverie.

He got up to stretch and found himself pacing non-stop. "Somehow I need to finance these orders. I need to get my long-term suppliers to extend enough credit to allow us to get through this weekend. Then on Monday I have to address some competitive bids. Two of our largest competitors are selling below cost — either to just stay in business or gain market share. They can't do that for long, unless they've figured out something we don't know yet. But the door is wide open to the Dutch roll-up firms who are buying out competitors. Of course, the longer-term crisis is the reality that close to 52 percent of our manufacturing client base has moved off-shore to lower labor markets.

"What we're doing is not working," Mitch said out loud with conviction. "We need a revolutionary new approach to survive." Then he countered himself.

"Yet our approach to organizational change has been widely accepted as the way to go about it. We've gathered the information, analyzed it, developed exhaustive reports, validated them and then made convincing company-wide presentations to get buy in. The case for change was clearly communicated to everyone before moving ahead. We identified the problems and solved them using a progressive methodology. Our teambuilding was thorough. We developed objectives and launched a change process that was designed to shift both mindsets and thinking processes."

Unhappily, Mitch admitted to himself that in spite of having instituted the new systems and controls, the concerns that motivated him to make the changes were still very much alive. "I don't feel like I have control over my own destiny anymore."

The Cost of Arrogance

AS HE CONTINUED TO PACE IN FRONT OF HIS LARGE EXECUTIVE DESK, Mitch mulled over his dilemma. "That's why I chose to leave GT in the first place. With all of the training they gave us I felt that I would have a real advantage over the other companies in my industry who simply didn't have the experience and education I had. Indeed, I believe I was right. I've bought out several competitors along the way. Ironically, none of the acquisitions have gone as planned. In spite of exhaustive due diligence, we've found things at every turn that we missed."

Mitch paused his pacing and let his gaze take in the magnificent view of lights from the skyline. Suddenly they became a blur. He rubbed his forehead, as if to clear his thinking. The thing that hit him so hard was that it seemed like something else was running the company. "Whatever it is, it has a life of its own. It's definitely not me," he said to no one. "It's something that's out of our control…and I just can't figure it out. I am not sure any CEO I have shared these thoughts with knows either. It's arrogant for any of us to think that we really have control. It sure is easy to think we're brilliant when things are going well and the economy is booming. Ironically, the wave we all rode in on — the booming economy (or whatever it was believed to be) was just a house of cards."

Shaking his head, Mitch returned to the comfort of his leather desk chair, realizing that even multiple audits hadn't caught what was wrong. In spite of feeling bone-tired, he managed a bit of sarcasm. "All that financial number crunching we do is like having someone with no real knowledge of automotive systems raise the hood of a car to see what is wrong."

UNHAPPILY, MITCH ADMITTED TO HIMSELF THAT IN SPITE OF
HAVING INSTITUTED THE NEW SYSTEMS AND CONTROLS,
THE CONCERNS THAT MOTIVATED HIM TO MAKE THE
CHANGES WERE STILL VERY MUCH ALIVE.

Not willing to let the issue go, Mitch's mind continued to deliberate. "There must be a way to actually determine how or why our company malfunctioned the way it has. For sure I can't predict how the people within it are going to perform. I've placed strong controls everywhere — in sales and marketing, personnel, production, inventory, forecasting and scheduling. Yet there is something else about our company that I don't seem to understand.

The Central Question: What is the Cause?

"I EXPECTED THE CONSULTING FIRMS WE HIRED TO SHED SOME LIGHT ON THINGS. I don't think they have a clue. The thing that no one can tell me is the actual cause of why things go wrong. Truthfully, I'm not sure I can even determine why we've been successful. I wonder what really determines success besides timing and location.

"I remember when I bought Bill's company; he really had something special going there. He had a deeper understanding of these things than the rest of us. When Bill chose not to stay on with the new team, things started to go downhill fast."

Although Mitch had sent his best manager to replace Bill, she was not able to keep the momentum and spirit alive. Some of his best people had since left, even though they were made attractive offers. It was puzzling to him why people left despite high unemployment and a limited job market. "Yet Bill's people seemed to have supreme confidence in where they were heading. In exit interviews they said things like 'I don't feel trusted.' They said they felt controlled, suppressed and fearful. They also said they were no longer considered valuable contributors. We've never heard that kind of feedback at exit interviews before. Strange."

Leaning all the way back with his hands behind his head, Mitch swiveled back and forth in his chair. "I wonder if Bill is still around and we could get together. He said to call him anytime I needed help or just wanted to talk. Maybe he's willing to come back and help in this crisis. I really did trust him, although I never understood him.

"I remember him saying that all he or anyone could really manage was where they placed their attention. The other thing he was working on — what did he call it — 'identifying the underlying structure that caused behavior. Cause is all that matters.' He really upset the executive team when he said we were looking in all the wrong places to correct what was going on. Something about leverage points…

"I think I'll take him up on his offer. I really need someone to talk to that can give me a different perspective. Where on earth is that note?"

Midway down in his Inbox, Mitch found the note:

Mitch,

There may come a time when you need someone to talk to. Based on some of the things I see happening, probably around October. Call me anytime.

Your friend,
Bill.

The Three Insights

FORGETTING ABOUT THE TIME, MITCH STARTED DIALING. When the phone rang, the answering service picked up and asked him to hold while the party was located. After a few seconds he heard, "Good morning, this is Bill."

"Bill? Hi — this is Mitchell Crandall. How are you? I guess I should ask where are you? You said good morning."

Bill laughed and said, "I'm in Wyoming and it is 1AM here. Where are you?"

"I am still in my office, Bill, trying to sort some things out. I reread your note and decided to call. I am sorry to call so late."

"No, not at all Mitch. I'm up writing, and have actually been thinking about you. As a matter of fact, I am trying to get my arms around what I saw happening in my old company after you acquired us. It's a real case study."

"What motivated that?"

"Well, I've been working with my mentor who helped me discover what I failed to make happen before I left you." After a pause, he continued, "So, what can I do for you, Mitch? I've been concerned about a possible crisis I saw coming this fall."

"Well, Bill, I don't know where else to turn right now. I've done everything I felt was right to move the company forward, but it's not working. We have really stalled. Now I'm facing a major financial and supplier crisis as well. You said to call anytime. I expected to get your answering service and see if we could find a time to get together and talk."

"Mitch, come on out to Wyoming. I'll be here another couple of weeks and then head back East to run sessions for the new company I've started."

"What is your new company, Bill?"

"It's called The Center for Inspired Performance. I'm in the process of finishing some mission-critical pieces for the series I'm running with several CEO groups back in Atlanta. Maybe you'd like to join us."

"Did you say a center for inspired performance? Bill, that's exactly what's missing in all the programs that I've implemented. It is clearly what you had going inside your firm when we bought it — inspired performance. I feel we somehow destroyed that spirit."

"Believe me when I tell you, Mitch, you did not destroy it. That spirit is still there, inside the people. It just needs to be released."

"What do you mean?" Mitch asked.

there are three insights that I learned from Willard, my mentor. ute for them?"

"You bet."

"Here are the Three Insights. You might want to jot them down.

The first is: *All things are energy.*

The second is: *Energy is never created or destroyed. It is just suppressed or released. It always takes the path of least resistance.*

The third is: *To change the flow of energy you need to change its underlying structure.*

"It took me some time to boil everything down and to understand all of this, and now I feel compelled to teach what I've learned to others. That's how I believe I'll really master it."

ENERGY IS NEVER CREATED OR DESTROYED.
IT IS JUST SUPPRESSED OR RELEASED.
IT ALWAYS TAKES THE PATH OF LEAST RESISTANCE.

As Mitch took notes on what Bill said (which he did during all his crucial conversations) he felt conflicted. All he could really think about was his crisis. "Bill, I would love to come out, but right now I am really in a bind. I need to take immediate action if I'm going to keep the doors open."

"What is the most critical thing that needs to be addressed? Maybe I can help."

"My suppliers are all in trouble and they have threatened not to ship if I can't produce a letter of credit on the parts I need. I'm extended at my bank; to make payroll last month I pledged my receivables to them. My customers have not paid according to their agreements. Now I am in a crisis situation."

"Look Mitch, why don't you email me who your suppliers are and what parts you need right away. If you don't mind, let me talk to them for you. I know all these guys. They were my suppliers as well, you know. Then, if you can't get out here, maybe you can plan to be at my first session on October fifteenth and we'll meet afterwards. Let's see if we can work together. We may not be able to, because of me leaving the company as I did, but we can sure try."

"Listen Bill, if we can get those parts in here and the orders shipped, maybe I could get out there for the weekend. Where is Wyoming, anyway? Just kidding. Listen, send me the details of where you are and let's talk later in the day. Is there anything I can do to prepare for our time together if I am able to join you out there?"

"Well, yes, there is. I have an organizational assessment I'd like you to fill out. I'm not sure where you'll find the time to do it — it requires a couple hours to complete. Maybe you can do it on the plane if everything works out for you to come."

"Thanks Bill. It's great talking to you. I somehow feel a little more relaxed. I'll let you go for now and email those suppliers to you along with their conditions for shipment. What's your email address?"

CHAPTER 2 *The Journey*

Mitch's plane landed on a small airstrip outside of Thermopolis, Wyoming. As he got off the plane and looked around, he saw a cowboy sitting on a horse just off to the side of the one room control tower. He had another horse beside him and waved with his hat for Mitch to come over. Mitch had worn his blue jeans and the cowboy boots he bought when skiing in Utah the last season. Now all he needed was a cowboy hat and he would have it all. "This is great," he thought. "Just what I need — to get away and really reflect on things. Maybe out here I can get a fresh perspective on how to approach the business."

Looking at the scenery all around, Mitch thought, "Wow, this is really great." Then he walked over and said "Hello" to the cowboy.

Tipping his hat the cowboy replied, "Mr. Crandall, Bill asked me to bring you to his place. I hope you can ride — it's the only way in and out. It will take us a couple of hours so we better get moving. By the way, Bill said to give you this hat. Hope it fits. Ready to ride?"

In spite of the beauty of the big sky all around him, Mitch's mind kept racing. "What worked before and got us to the size and rate of growth that we achieved, now seems to be coming full circle and biting us in the anatomy," he thought pensively. "No doubt that our pricing and go-to-market strategies have been aggressive. Maybe too aggressive. It sure got us market share, which is what we were after if we were going to take the firm public and raise more capital," he ruminated. Suddenly realizing what he was doing, Mitch decided to just relax and take things as they came.

"This is great. I just love it," he affirmed to himself. "Way out in Wyoming. How long has it been since I just picked up and went somewhere like this? Especially right now. I have been at it 16 hours a day for months, trying to put out one fire after another."

The cowboy didn't speak for close to an hour. Then he pulled up and asked Mitch to notice what he saw all around him. Mitch looked, but didn't know how to reply. What he had been enjoying as he rode had now, somehow, become a study, a test. As he looked around he commented on the incredible beauty of what he saw. The cowboy simply said, "Look deeper, Mr. Crandall." Then very softly he said, "Deeper," and gently motioned to his horse to ride on.

For a long time Mitch reflected on the cowboy's question, knowing that he was clearly missing something. What did he mean, to look deeper? Then he noticed with a start that the cowboy had disappeared out of sight on the trail. "Which way did he go?" Mitch pondered, eyes widening. "Where did he go?" Mitch felt a little edge of fear creeping in. "I came out here to meet with Bill and talk business strategy; now I'm thrust into an entirely new situation I didn't see coming at all. First there was what seemed like a simple question about what I saw, and now I'm uncertain what direction to go. Surely the cowboy will realize that I was not close behind and return for me. Perhaps I should just wait here until he comes back."

After a few moments, Mitch dug his heels into the side of the horse wanting to see if he could catch up with his guide. He felt alone and a mild panic set in. It was a feeling that he often had in running the business, even when he was in the middle of a board meeting with his directors and senior management.

Without the cowboy leading the way, he realized that this was really wild country. "Where did my guide go?" As he rode forward, he soon came to what appeared to be a junction in the path. One path seemed most often taken, the other was very subtle. Actually it was difficult to make out. Unless you knew about it or were watching for it, you would miss it, Mitch realized.

He also admitted that if he were just following his guide he definitely would not have noticed this path. "I wonder how much I miss because I'm locked into following my way of doing things," Mitch reflected.

He checked his watch and realized that it had been almost twenty minutes since he had lost sight of the cowboy. "How could this have happened? I guess he wasn't aware that I wasn't behind him, but by now that should have been obvious to him. This is really frustrating. I was searching for the answer to what had become a riddle and now I'm lost and alone in this country where I'm uncertain about which way to go. I don't have a road map, a compass or any instructions."

Then Mitch remembered that the cowboy said "You could only get into and out of Bill's place on horseback." The one path was clearly more traveled and led to an open valley below. There were tire tracks visible and a road far below to the right. He would be able to see his guide if he had gone in that direction. Normally he would take the well-beaten path — the one that seemed safe, tested, easily visible. Maybe he should take the path less traveled.

Mitch pulled at the reigns, jerking his horse to the left. It responded immediately and lunged forward with a surge of energy. He suddenly felt adventuresome in a way that he had not felt in years. "This is rather exciting. I feel free — and alive. I know Bill would not just leave me out here, unless he expected me to learn something. Maybe this is why he wanted me to come all the way out to Wyoming."

His mind was racing, but he was acutely aware of everything around him. His consciousness had shifted into super drive. He was looking for signs of tracks now, and before long he clearly saw new hoof marks in the dirt along with some fresh horse dung. He felt relief that he was obviously on the right path and following his guide. "Strange how I labeled this unnamed cowboy my guide," he thought. "That makes him a lot more important in my life right now than he was an hour ago."

"THIS IS RATHER EXCITING. I FEEL FREE — AND ALIVE. I KNOW BILL WOULD NOT JUST LEAVE ME OUT HERE, UNLESS HE EXPECTED ME TO LEARN SOMETHING. MAYBE THIS IS WHY HE WANTED ME TO COME ALL THE WAY OUT TO WYOMING."

But what was most important was watching for any markers or signs. He needed to be acutely aware of every movement on the unmarked trail…the one he had chosen. How often had he missed signals that would have told him he was getting into trouble? "I'm sure there were indicators that would have told me all of these problems were coming if I was looking for them," he reflected.

"What did Bill mean that he had seen this crisis coming in October?"

Mitch pondered. "Why was he thinking about me at the time I called Wednesday evening? How was he able to make a few phone calls and suddenly have his old suppliers willing to ship immediately without any special rush order charges? To be truthful," Mitch acknowledged to himself, "what they delivered was far superior in quality to what we've been using. It was really world class. I haven't utilized that level of parts quality in some time." Mitch knew this had cost him in warranty claims, but that was 'the cost of doing business.' At least that is what he thought when his people came up with new lower-cost suppliers. He saved close to 30 percent.

"When Bill picked up the phone and called his old suppliers," Mitch recalled, "they really responded. They were clearly focused on serving us. They shared ideas that immediately cut our assembly costs and delivery times. Everyone could see the higher quality parts were easier to use and achieved a tighter fit. Our people were really astonished with the quality of service these suppliers provided. They completely saved the day, and even stayed with us during assembly to make sure that we knew how to properly implement their ideas. It energized everyone. Where we were short-hand-ed, due to labor cuts, they pitched in and helped out. They were there late working with us until the orders were out the door. But most impressive, none of them were managers; they were front-line workers.

"It was really inspiring. I was there, working right alongside them. It was quite emotional to see us go from the very brink of disaster to a very successful delivery. One more little unexpected miracle, but we're far from out of the woods. We were just able to make payroll one more time, that's all. But it seemed like we accomplished something more."

He recalled one of the three insights that Bill had shared on the phone Wednesday evening, that energy is neither created nor destroyed, just sup-pressed or released. Clearly the people from SynergyCorp had released the energy of their workforce.

As Mitch carefully made his way along the trail, he began to understand what the guide meant with his question. He could now see how everything in nature seemed to be in balance.

"So what do I notice around me here in the wilderness? 'Look deeply,' the cowboy had said. "I'm beginning to see things that I don't think I could have seen if I were following him. I've never thought about the way nature is in complete balance before. If the guide had been leading the way I would have just been following him mindlessly."

The more Mitch looked around the more he could see how everything seemed to work together as he made his way along the path. It had been that way forever. Then he thought, "Perhaps the same is true for my company — that there's a complete system serving us in the same manner." Although Bill had said things like that during one of their conversations, Mitch had not understood what he was talking about. Now he was beginning to. Clearly they had upset the balance of nature by taking the well-traveled pathway of cutting costs and playing one vendor against another to get the lowest price. Now he could see that those short-term gains ended up costing him dearly.

"This all reminds me of my old scoutmaster who would ask us questions when we were on overnight campouts and then leave us alone to discover the answers. He never gave us the answers or even told us if we were right or wrong. Similarly," Mitch recalled, "Bill never tried to change us when he was still with us after the merger, although he did state on several occasions that we were violating specific principles and not making — or was it living by — what he called fundamental choices.

"None of us understood what he was trying to say. Several of the senior managers took his comments personally. Truthfully, we were somewhat glad to see him leave. We thought it would allow us to mold his company to be the way we wanted it to be. We felt we could get it to operate according to our methods and way of doing things. Instead," he admitted, "we upset the balance and momentum that Bill said he was carefully trying to maintain.

"Last night, one of the workers from SynergyCorp said something that startled me as I was thanking them after the last box was on the truck and ready to be shipped. He said, 'No, Mr. Crandall, thank you for our being able to, in some small way, repay Bill for all he has done to help us see ourselves as contributors, not just employees working for a pay check.' He also said that the assembly ideas we implemented were his own. He was thrilled to see them actually working.

"What had Bill done," Mitch wondered, "that made such an impact on one of his suppliers and caused one of their front-line workers to be so grateful?"

Even though Mitch was barely making his way through the wilderness, he was seeing things that he had never noticed — not just on the trail, but in all areas of his life. Was he reflecting deeply, as the cowboy suggested? That he wasn't sure of yet, but he definitely was aware of thinking on a completely different level. "A single question can be very powerful if you let it in," he acknowledged. "It is certainly far more powerful than just presenting data to people and using it to convince them of what to do."

As Mitch continued along the path, rather comforted that he was progressing and heading in the right direction, he was suddenly paralyzed with fear. He had come to the edge of a cliff, with absolutely nowhere to go. Had he, in fact, taken the wrong path? Was this some sort of a test? "I have been afraid of heights for as long as I can recall," he admitted to himself, "ever since I looked over the side of Coolidge Dam when I was seven. It felt like I was going to fall over, but at the same time I had the urge to jump. It was an overwhelming sensation. Looking over the edge of this cliff gives me the exact same feeling." A cold sweat drenched his face.

But there he was, faced with another choice. It seemed impossible to turn around, and he wasn't a good enough horseman to back a horse up under these circumstances. Mitch took a deep breath and it seemed to ease his fright. Just up from the path he noticed a rope bridge spanning the chasm to the other side. More choices to ponder. "Should I get off and walk the horse along the cliff edge to the bridge and attempt to get to the other side? I feel safe on the horse. Am I really on the right path? Surely there is a sign that will provide me with direction and give me some assurance that I should proceed or that I need to head back."

At this point Mitch was no longer looking for the guide. He was clearly on his own. Reluctantly he got off the horse, which he had come to rely on, knowing he must now guide it. As he turned up the path towards the bridge and stepped out from the trees, suddenly there was

a clearing. His cowboy guide was patiently sitting there. He didn't say anything. Just nodded appreciatively.

The Power of Focus

AFTER A MOMENT OR TWO THE COWBOY BROKE THE SILENCE. "Bill has lunch ready — just across the ravine. We'll leave the horses here in the stall until we head back on Monday." He took Mitch's horse and brushed it down, whispering gently in its ear. Then he turned and said he had a fear of heights and that he had learned to choose a place on the other side and focus on it when crossing the ravine. He suggested it might work for Mitch as well. Then without any further discussion the cowboy started across.

Once he was on the other side, Mitch took a few steps and was immediately flooded with fear. He panicked. On one level he was completely aware that it was possible to do this, but everything in his being kept him from moving. He was paralyzed, just as he had been as a child. He heard the cowboy say, "Focus, Mr. Crandall, just focus and walk. After you start, keep moving."

Mitch took a deep breath. "Find a spot and focus on it," he told himself. "Then just keep moving forward." He found a knot on the tree ahead and instantaneously, at the moment that he was completely focused on it, everything else disappeared. He only saw the knot on the tree where the rope bridge was attached. He took a single step, but found his hand would not let go of the rope. Then the cowboy said, "Let go, Mr. Crandall. Just let go." Following his advice, Mitch almost had to pry his hand loose. With the next step he was suddenly moving effortlessly to the other side, calm and exhilarated at the same time.

The power of focus was quite astounding. Mitch could not remember ever being so intensely focused that everything around him disappeared. He felt like he was literally being drawn to that one spot. He felt attached to it completely…like a lifeline. All his fear was replaced with a sense of peace. "If I can handle this, by simply focusing, what else could I have achieved? More importantly, what else can I achieve!" Suddenly, Mitch felt a surge of energy.

Then he reflected on what he had failed to accomplish due to lack of focus. "What situations have I avoided due to a lack of awareness or fear? I've been so distracted for the longest time. Since we implemented our growth strategy, I've handled multiple problems on a daily basis. I can see that I have never had this level of totally conscious focus in my business. What would be possible if I were to determine what to focus on that would accomplish the kind of results I really wanted? What have I been holding onto that has kept me from moving forward? What if my entire team had this level of conscious focus? What do we need to let go of?" Again, Mitch was energized with the thought of discovering the answers to these questions.

> "WHAT WOULD BE POSSIBLE IF I WERE TO DETERMINE WHAT TO FOCUS ON THAT WOULD ACCOMPLISH THE KIND OF RESULTS I REALLY WANTED?"

The cowboy held out his hand as Mitch stepped down from the bridge. He said to go on ahead and meet Bill. He would be along shortly. First, he wanted to implement an idea that came to him when crossing the ravine, one he thought would strengthen the bridge — especially during stormy weather. Mitch watched as he took a deep breath, got focused, and walked to the center of the rope bridge. The cowboy began to reinforce it directly in the middle, where the stress was the greatest. He remembered how it had swayed back and forth when he walked over it and that there was at least a 1000-foot drop to the bottom of the ravine. Mitch admitted to himself, "I don't think I'm ready for that yet."

As he watched the cowboy out there — concerned that he would lose his balance — Mitch was once again overwhelmed with panic and fear. "I wonder how much of what I have done has been out of fear. One thing I know for sure is that our entire organization has not been focused and fear has been our main motivator."

Ownership

WATCHING HIM IMPLEMENT HIS IDEAS, IT WAS CLEAR TO MITCH that the cowboy felt complete ownership of the bridge. From Mitch's point of view, he was risking his life out there. But from the cowboy's perspective, he suspected, he was saving lives. He moved easily and effortlessly as he went about reinforcing the bridge and taking the pressure off each of the twisted ropes in the center. Clearly he was making the bridge stronger in all the right places. Then he stood, took a deep breath, recaptured his focus and moved forward to the far side of the bridge. Once there, he did some additional reinforcing and the sway in the bridge stopped. Mitch wondered if the cowboy made corrections every time he crossed the bridge. He suspected that was true regarding everything he did.

As Mitch started up the path to the lodge, he hoped to gain some clarity from Bill on his recent musings. Then, he remembered the three insights. They were all about energy, how you release it or suppress it — how it follows the path of least resistance, and that to change it you need to change the underlying structure over which it flows. "Perhaps that's what I did by focusing on the knothole on the tree as I walked across the ravine," Mitch thought with a new lightness in his step. "I literally changed the underlying structure of my thinking by placing my attention on the knothole. This is what allowed me to cross."

Following the path about another 100 yards, Mitch stepped into an opening that had the most spectacular view. Bill's place overlooked an entire valley and was surrounded by a cliff. It was like nothing he had ever seen before. A dog barked and started running toward him as Bill came out the door to greet him. "Welcome, Mitch! Let's go inside, have something to eat, and get reacquainted." "Great," Mitch replied.

"How was your horse?" Bill asked. "She is a great ride isn't she?" Mitch smiled and nodded. "Did you have any trouble finding the place?" Bill said with a hearty chuckle that seemed to come from deep inside him. Mitch started to laugh just as heartily. It had been a long time since he had laughed like that. "You're hungry, I hope?"

As they ate, Mitch said, "Bill, I had an incredible experience on the journey up here and feel like I learned a lot about myself."

"Tell me what you discovered."

Mitch related his growing level of awareness on the trail, the power of focus on the bridge — having to let go, and the degree of ownership that the cowboy displayed in caring for the bridge.

Nodding his head in agreement, Bill said, "This place and the journey up here often have that effect on people." After a few moments, he added, "It is all about being reflective and open to learning. When people are so certain of their own ideas they can't see what you have discovered, Mitch. Personally, I've never come up here when it didn't require my total attention and focus — especially in rough weather or in the middle of winter when the winds come howling down the canyon and the trail is icy. That's when the bridge really becomes treacherous."

Lunch never tasted so good. Mitch felt light inside, yet grounded. What had happened on the way up here?

"Mitch, it's so great to have you here. This is a very special place to me. I come here when I need to regain my perspective. It's where I can reflect on a deep level. Being here helps me clarify my focus, like you said."

"How did you find such a place? It's amazing!"

"It was pledged to me by the Indian tribal council that owns all of the rights to the land out here. It's a sacred place where shaman from the surrounding tribes used to gather to become spiritually aligned. I'm humbled to be able to be here and share it with others. That's all the tribal council and the chief asked of me when they pledged it to me. The chief said the energy present here is available only to those who are willing to give it to others. They said they had a vision that it be used to serve leaders who are committed to serving their people and communities in an inspired way.

"When you look out from here you can see their entire land. On a clear day you really can see forever. Several times a year the tribal council and I meet here to address council issues and the destiny of their people. They are faced with great challenges as a nation, even greater than when the white men ran them off their land.

"That's why I asked you to come out here instead of us meeting in Atlanta. I hope you don't mind too much. I know it required changing your schedule during a very challenging time for you and your company. Thank you so much, Mitch. I am honored to be able to serve you in some small way."

CHAPTER 3 *Overcoming Organizational Blindness and the Reactive State*

Pushing his chair back to face Mitch directly, Bill continued. "Before we go too much further, it would help me to know what past experiences you may have had with me that caused any barriers or difficulties in our past relationship."

Mitch thought for some time, a little stunned by the nature of the question. Then he said, "You know Bill, there was a time when we either didn't understand you at all or felt threatened by the things you said to us. Especially about violating principles or not running the business according to fundamental choices. What did all that mean? I still don't know, but I do know that I didn't have a clue what you were talking about and resisted what you were saying."

Communication is Determined by Where You Come From

"MITCH, THE TRUTH IS THAT I DIDN'T KNOW HOW TO TALK ABOUT what I was learning so that others could possibly comprehend what I was practicing. I had a teacher, but was far from being one myself. Now I'm finally learning how to learn in a way that I can communicate it to others. This has required an entire shift in where I come from. I know that what I did and said drove you and others away from me. I sure made it difficult for us to work together."

"Well, that's true. You know, Bill, we were somewhat relieved when you decided to leave, so we could remake your company in our own more "corporate" image. Now I realize that we dismantled what you had built — instead of discovering what it was that made your company so effective and profitable, and then replicating it throughout our organization. I admit, at the time we were taking advantage of the purchasing leverage we had gained with our suppliers and optimizing our marketing advantages. I thought we were focused, but probably on all of the wrong things."

"Well," Bill replied, "I know that I caused a lot of emotional tension for you and your senior managers. Although I had created something really valuable in my company, I was unable to share it with you in a way that you could use it. That's the real reason I left, Mitch. I needed to master the principles that I had been applying but didn't know how to share them with others. This has been my singular pursuit."

Organizational Blindness and the Reactive State

"WHAT MADE YOU FEEL THAT WE COULDN'T UNDERSTAND what you were saying to us, Bill?"

"Initially, I was frustrated by my inability to communicate. I was creating resistance. I could feel it. Then I realized I was trying to share something that couldn't be seen. Very simply, I realized that unless high performance and productivity could be seen, there was never a chance for anyone to experience it or feel it.

"Mitch, you wanted to address everything on an analytical or thinking level. I was trying to get across what I saw and felt. Your way made perfect sense. I could not debate you on it. It was totally logical. It just didn't work — for me or for my people, at least. It became the source of a lot of anxiety. My people felt judged and evaluated and became fearful of making mistakes.

"I've had a lot of time to work with change since I left the company. I think for change to really take hold and stick over time, everyone has to see it and feel it. It is more of a heart thing than a head thing. I tried to place seeing and feeling things into an analytical model for you, and failed."

Sounding on a more positive note, Bill continued. "But, since then, I've developed a name for it. It's called *organizational blindness*…and I think I've figured out how to address it." As he poured them both another glass of iced tea, Bill pointed out that organizational blindness, when coupled with being caught in an out-of-balance state, results in unwanted surprises or events. "This causes (and reinforces) a *reactive state* — where it is impossible to see what's going on around you or hear what others are saying. When reacting," he continued to point out, "you are in *survival mode* for that moment of time. When you are in survival mode, it is very difficult to stay focused. That is one of the great managerial dilemmas."

Clarity of Focus Comes From Within

"BILL, BY CROSSING THE BRIDGE TODAY I ACHIEVED SOMETHING I thought was impossible. I realize I have stayed away from heights since a really negative early childhood experience. I have no idea how many other things I've been avoiding due to fears and dislikes. Talk about reacting — both my management team and I have been totally consumed by upset conditions in the firm. We have been fire fighting and calling it problem solving, haven't we?" Not waiting for an answer, Mitch continued. "Are you saying that one of the principles we violated has to do with focus?"

"Clarity of Focus may seem like a simple principle, and it is. But being able to truly harness the power of focus is mission critical. It comes from within. Look at what focus allowed you to accomplish when crossing the bridge this morning. I'm glad your journey up here had a powerful impact on you."

As Mitch thought further, he realized he was able to make the transfer of his personal avoidance style to the behavior of his organization. He could see other glaring examples of reaction and avoidance such as not confronting head-on fears or emotional upsets. "We avoided them without even knowing that's what we were doing," he thought to himself. Then he related to Bill how things had become like an out-of-control virus inside the company, and acknowledged how much that had restricted everyone's ability to learn and grow, both personally and organizationally.

The Power of Principles

"THE PRINCIPLE OF FOCUS IS SO POWERFUL THAT IT LITERALLY DETERMINES what you produce. When your focus is on what gets your attention or anything else you don't want, you end up with more of that… More of what you don't want. Quite a paradox, don't you think?" Bill added, shaking his head and smiling. "When you violate a principle it exacerbates or multiplies whatever you are trying to resolve. Stated another familiar way, whatever you avoid or resist persists. It grows. You will produce whatever you focus on. That's true even when it's something you don't want or are trying to get rid of.

"The thing about all principles," Bill continued, "is that they work both ways — just as clarity of focus does. Principles don't care. They work whether you're aware of them or not. And they work unceasingly, all the time. They never quit."

As Bill continued, he pointed out to Mitch that principles operate in such a manner that the "fires" as he called them, keep getting bigger until you finally discover whatever principle it is that you are violating. He explained that you could be trying to improve something and at the same time be violating a principle and destroying the very thing you are trying to improve. He emphasized that many organizations end up in one crisis after another. Then everyone suffers — and the difficulties are amplified. "That's why understanding the three insights is essential. Everything flows from them, so you must be grounded in them."

> THE THING ABOUT ALL PRINCIPLES . . . IS THAT
> THEY WORK BOTH WAYS. PRINCIPLES DON'T CARE. THEY
> WORK WHETHER YOU'RE AWARE OF THEM OR NOT.

"Now I can see what you were talking about when you said we were violating principles, Bill. What other principles did you see us violating?"

"First, it might be a good idea to think about what you choose to focus on, Mitch. What gets your personal attention?"

"That's easy. It's on what is not going according to plan. It is what's behind schedule or over budget. It is all of the unplanned surprises."

"Let's see if we can map out what you do when those things take place. Generally there is a breakdown of some kind, right?"

"Right. That signals to me that something is out of control. There is a lack of accountability, communications or managerial controls, or systems not being followed."

"What do you do when that happens?"

"We meet and focus on getting it back into control."

"How do you get it back under control?"

"We review it and see where someone did not meet expectations. We either clarify and reinforce existing controls or develop and implement new ones."

"Mitch, when you implement controls, does it create a feeling of trust or distrust?"

"Never thought about it that way Bill, but the answer is distrust. I know when someone tries to control me I become very resistant, even angry."

"So what happens to people's energy? Remember the three insights? Energy cannot be destroyed; it can only be released or suppressed."

"Well, I guess feeling controlled and distrusted suppresses energy."

"Let's assume that everyone is creative. When their energy is suppressed, how does it come out — especially when feeling controlled? You were in the military, Mitch, what did people do?"

"They would beat the system — reinforcing the need for more controls. But that's what the chain of command is all about."

"Absolutely! In an organization, however, it becomes a vicious circle, taking on a life of its own. This can result in silos, politics or various forms of conflict. People look out for themselves — protecting their budgets, resources, or trying to gain a personal advantage. It also results in self-serving behavior and game playing. People blame each other, make excuses and try to justify why they didn't get things accomplished."

Reaching for a legal pad, Bill continued, "Here's what that looks like when we map it out.

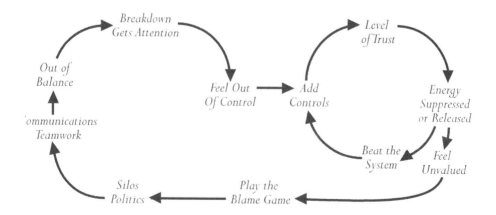

"Energy, in this case, takes the path of least resistance and ends up causing even more breakdowns. Do you see where this further reinforces the need for more controls?"

Mitch nodded thoughtfully.

"If we don't understand this simple loop diagram," Bill emphasized, "it keeps getting repeated. People become frustrated, disengaged, feel unvalued or marginalized. They don't want to contribute or try new things to improve their performance. Worst-case scenario, the creative high performers leave while those who are not, stay. Those who stay seem to only care about their paycheck, survival, or protecting their little fiefdom. Of course, communication, teamwork, trust, shared knowledge and innovation get sucked down the drain — along with their energy."

"So, Bill, this is what you mean when you say that energy cannot be destroyed — just released or suppressed. When it is suppressed, it comes out in totally counterproductive ways.

"I can see how this exact scenario took place with two of the companies we acquired and tried to merge into our way of doing things. We eventually had to remove the current management and put our own in place. This has become our worst nightmare. What we did to gain a foothold in those markets ended up sucking up all kinds of cash and resources. In addition, many of the problems we acquired were not discovered during our rather exhaustive due diligence. It has taken a couple of years to clean up some of these messes. What's the alternative?"

The Single Aim of an Organization

"LET'S NOT MOVE TOO FAST, MITCH. LET'S FOCUS AND GET CLARITY FIRST. *The single aim of any organization is to place the right amount of focus, attention or pressure on just the right place for the right amount of time in order to achieve the desired amount of movement.* Willard, my mentor, calls where we place our attention **leverage points**. However, only when you see and are dealing with **'causality'** is it possible to discover your leverage points."

Mitch jumped in, "That description of an organization's aim is quite a mouthful. But as you know, I think it's management's job to maximize the value of all assets. You know how bottom-line focused I am. I won't move on anything unless I can see the payback — and I'm more willing to be long-term focused than most CEOs today. I think I just heard you say that maximizing assets is accomplished by focusing our attention on leverage points. But I am not sure what a leverage point is. How do you identify what they are? And where is the bottom line?"

Defining the Generative Organization

"THE ULTIMATE DILEMMA THAT CONFRONTS CEOs IS CHOOSING between creating a Generative Organization or merely surviving in a reactive one. *Focusing on leverage points is totally generative, as opposed to reactive.*" Bill approached Mitch's questions by explaining that *leverage points remove the source of upset conditions and the limits to growth.*

He emphasized that you know when you are not working with high-leverage points because what you're doing tends to create more upset and results in reacting to events. And a bottom-line focus can actually be the cause of those upset conditions and limits to growth. "In both the long run and the short run it will lower asset value — not maximize it."

"Well, choosing to build a generative organization seems a good choice. Reacting is not what I would call making a choice. It makes for late nights, anxiety, and some very unhappy people. Me included," Mitch said with a weak smile. "Can you give me a thumbnail sketch of what it takes to build a generative organization? You are introducing a whole new concept to me right now."

"*Generative means having the power of producing, or originating.* Imagine that a river is flowing along and we need to harness its power to provide electricity for the valley below. What would you do?"

"Now you are in my universe, Bill. Electrical engineering was my major at MIT. I actually worked on the construction of the Yellowtail Dam outside of Hardin, Montana, for a couple of summers. The simple description is that you dam up the river, and then build systems that transform the power of the river by using massive turbines. Apply a few very basic principles of power generation and electricity, and you will have enough electrical capacity for the entire population of Montana and the surrounding region."

"That's exactly what we mean when we focus on building a Generative Organization, Mitch. Obviously, it takes a lot of design skills, engineering know-how, the application of organizing principles, strategic thinking and

managerial discipline to pull it off. For our purposes, for an organization to achieve its objectives and single aim, it needs to become truly generative."

"That is quite a shift from being reactive," Mitch acknowledged. "Where do you suggest we start?"

The Six Strategies and Managerial Disciplines

"Strategically, Mitch, strategically! We have to start by thinking and executing strategically. So the first thing we do is follow a process that is like the turbine in the dam, so to speak. This turbine engine is a constant truing mechanism that follows a process of Assess, Design, Align, and Execute. It's a feedback control process utilizing a Navigational Guidance System like we use to constantly manage the dynamic nature of an organization."

"Ok Bill, I like that. I am certainly more comfortable when you talk strategy. That, I understand."

Bill nodded, then continued, "In building a generative organization, everything is based on Strategic Execution in Six Focus Areas. Each strategy requires the development of very specific competencies. Ultimately, being generative results in becoming a competency-development organization.

"Let me give you an overview of the focus areas. I'm sure they'll resonate with you, knowing how strongly you believe in strategy. As a matter of fact, I've prepared a few 'dashboards' which indicate where your organization is right now, based on the Organizational Assessment you completed before coming out here. I was amazed you got that done."

"Me too," Mitch chuckled.

Picking up his legal pad, Bill wrote: 1. Leadership Effectiveness, 2. Sales Effectiveness, 3. Customer Enthusiasm, 4. Employee Inspiration, 5. Productive Capacity, 6. Competitive Advantage.

"Each strategy has six critical competencies that need to be developed — basically made up of 'best practices.' Our goal is to achieve balance between the six strategies and the long-term focus of becoming a competency based, best practices company.

"Here are the results from your Assessment. They will provide you with a base line for being strategically focused. Your total leadership effectiveness is made up of six competencies.

"The first one is **Leadership Effectiveness**. The area in the middle shows where you believe your organization is operating at the present time. Looks like you are pretty tough on yourself, Mitch. You are right on the edge of being a really good company."

Mitch's Combined **Leadership Effectiveness**: Good

Vision Mission Values
Is 66.4%

Team Management
Is 70.2%

Strategic Execution
is 67.3%

Employee Alignment
Is 69.5%

Managerial Discipline
70.6%

Organizational Design
Is 60.1%

60%   70%   80%   90%

Great   Best   Good   Reactive   In Business   Leadership Effectiveness

"The next one addresses the competencies required for achieving your **Sales Effectiveness** goals. This one really drills down to the best practices that result in maximizing your go-to-market strategy."

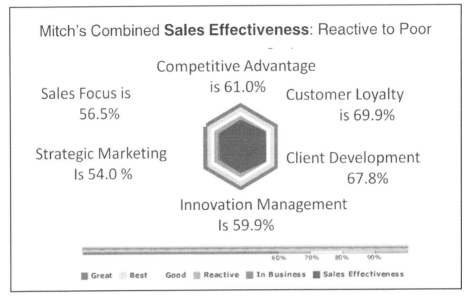

"**Customer Enthusiasm** gets to the issues that provide a real foundation for growing your business based on referrals and customer objectives being met."

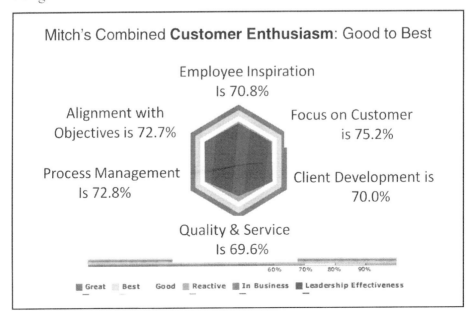

"Fundamentally, though, everything is rooted in **Employee Inspiration**. You simply must have the right people in the right jobs, capable of doing the right things, with consistent, immediate and accurate feedback. This results in them going beyond their best past performance."

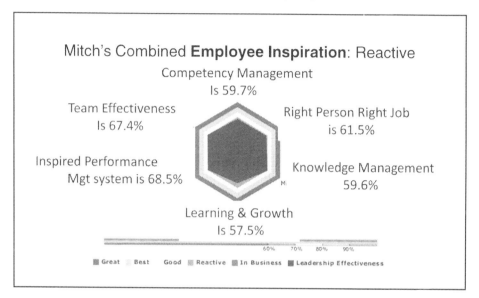

"**Productive Capacity** is all about maximizing your resources based on each person's capability to contribute."

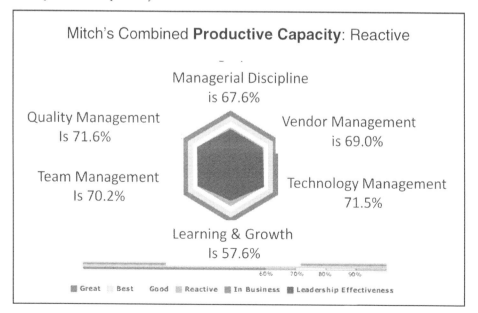

"And finally, all of this adds up to achieving a **Competitive Advantage**. Ironically, very few organizations even scratch the surface in doing what it takes to achieve in this most strategic focus area. It is not something that gets your attention until competition has passed you by."

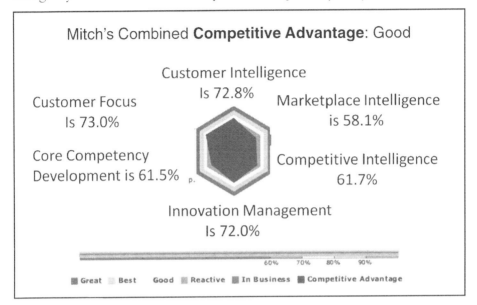

"Mitch, I can tell you were really brutal on yourself when you completed the assessments."

"You know Bill, until I had to face each one of these questions and ask how far along we were in terms of actual implementation, I would have said we had to be up there in the Great category. That is certainly how I rated myself after I completed Jim Collins' book, *Good to Great*. But I did your survey after watching SynergyCorp show up and assure our delivery on Friday. That was a sobering moment for me. I could see a huge difference between them and us. It helped me realize how far we have to go in each one of these areas. This visual data makes it very easy for us to benchmark our development. It was tough to take the time to complete the assessments, but without them we would not know where we are and be able to track our development. I will definitely use this data in the strategic planning process we'll be going through in the next couple of months."

Grabbing his pad again, Bill explained that the execution of these strategies requires managerial discipline in six areas: 1. Performance Management, 2. Process Management, 3. Project Management, 4. Knowledge Management, 5. Resource Management, and 6. Change Management. I've prepared the results from your assessments on these as well. I think they will add to your planning process by pinpointing the areas that you need to focus on in order to execute your strategic plan."

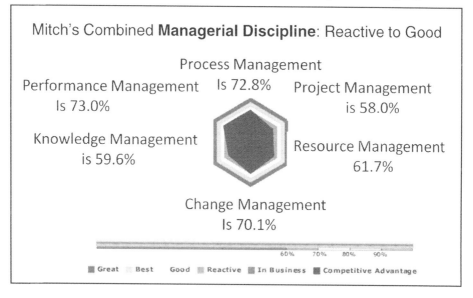

"You know, I have never had a snapshot of exactly where we are in any of these strategic areas or management practices before. What I think happens to us — and other organizations — is that we get caught up in the reactive loop you mapped out. It is very difficult to maintain focus on the developmental skills we need in order to change the way the company operates.

"Our approach to performance management, for example, boils down to annual performance reviews, and that was our highest score out of all of these. I have a few good project managers, but they tell me they are unable to utilize their skills in this area because we are constantly jerking them around in a fire fighting mode all over the company. I guess we do that to them because they are our best people. This is certainly not a good report card I am looking at," Mitch said with a frown. "Nobody wants this kind of news. I think I have had a tendency to kill the messengers inside the company when they tried to deliver this kind of data to me in the past."

The Truing Process: Assess, Design, Align and Execute

RISING TO STRETCH A BIT MITCH OFFERED, "Now, my guess is that this is where your truing process of Assess, Design, Align and Execute comes in. I will constantly need to go through the truing process focused on execution in these six strategic areas. Very similar to Edward Deming's Plan-Do-Check-Act Model to achieve Quality."

"Exactly, Mitch. Actually every person in the organization keeps score, based on goals linked directly to each of the strategies and corresponding competencies."

"So this is how the Navigational Guidance System keeps the company focused. It allows you to make course corrections as you move into the future. To do that, wouldn't it have to work sort of like a sonar control feedback loop? One that would guide us to our destination and would help us achieve strategic objectives? It looks like being generative takes a 'total systems' approach to organizational growth. Am I following you?"

Leading Indicators and the Navigational Guidance System

"YOU'RE RIGHT ON, MITCH. The Navigational Guidance System, or the NGS. does exactly what you described. It works like a sonar system sending out signals that give you feedback about what's coming in the future. With this data, you can make strategic corrections and become totally predictive. It's an enterprise-wide performance management system based on 'leading indicators'… and it certainly is a total systems approach to controlling your destiny."

Moving back to his seat at the table, Mitch asked for clarification. "Bill, what you have just described does not exist anywhere that I know of. How do you achieve the sonar effect? Precisely what do you mean when you talk about 'leading indicators'?"

"Right now the system you have is based on your financials and other sources of data that indicate the condition of the organization. Right? They're tied into your expenses, costs, inventory, sales revenue and other financials to indicate your profitability for the month. Those are all **lagging indicators**. So, Mitch, how long does it take for you to know how you are actually performing each month?"

"Well, actually, the time lag is getting shorter, but it always comes after the books are closed. I guess that is what you mean by lagging indicators."

"You bet," Bill affirmed. He emphasized that to be truly generative requires a feedback system based on principles that allow you to control your organizational destiny. To accomplish this, the guidance system provides daily scorekeeping that gives immediate and consistent feedback, allowing you to be predictive and make the necessary corrections to avoid fires. "It's also designed so everyone is focused on going beyond their best past performance. Collectively that leads to the overall growth of your enterprise."

"Where do you get this kind of data? How do you know how to use it to make it predictive?"

"It starts by looking at each strategic focus area separately. Once we understand the underlying structure that determines how that area performs, we can identify leverage points, resulting in a balanced state of growth. Then we connect them all together to get the predictive result you are asking about."

"THE GUIDANCE SYSTEM PROVIDES DAILY SCOREKEEPING THAT GIVES IMMEDIATE AND CONSISTENT FEEDBACK, ALLOWING YOU TO BE PREDICTIVE AND MAKE NECESSARY CORRECTIONS. . ."

"I want to know how this is possible, Bill."

"Tell you what, Mitch. The first thing we'll do is map out the underlying structure of one of your strategic focus areas. Then you'll be able to see exactly what we're talking about. Once we have the underlying structure we'll be able to identify the leverage points that will result in attaining a balanced state of growth."

Mitch looked Bill directly in the eyes. "When do we start?"

Developing Vision: The Ability to See

"THE CRITICAL THING IS TO BE ABLE TO SEE AND OVERCOME organizational blindness," Bill responded. "The way we do that is to start with what we can, in fact, see," he continued, rising and heading toward a conference table, made from native hard woods, at the other end of the large room. "Generally, what is visible is what gets your attention. So let's start by identifying the events or surprises that have been getting your attention."

As Mitch came over to join him, Bill continued, "Then we'll take the first step in overcoming organizational blindness by charting the patterns that surround the events. This is done in the form of a timeline," he emphasized "so that you can see the impact of these patterns over time."

Pulling out a chair to sit at the conference table, Mitch clarified his situation. "Most of the time we're dealing with problems. If something is wrong, it's a problem that must be solved. I know that's what we've been doing. We even reward problem solvers for their ability to do whatever it takes to service the customer. We pride ourselves on that, as you know. Our customer service mission statement is: Do whatever it takes to satisfy the customer."

Taking a seat next to Mitch, Bill responded, "That's one of the reasons I was willing to sell my company to you. It was your total commitment to taking care of your customers. That's what I really admired about you. However, when I charted the effect of doing "whatever it took" to take care of a single customer's concerns, I discovered they were just quick fixes that resulted in longer-term, downstream difficulties, and other clients would always suffer."

Looking Mitch kindly in the eyes, Bill shared the painful truth that doing "whatever it took" impacted his inventory, delivery times, forecasting, scheduling and billing accuracy. He explained how it also caused upset in how resources were allocated company-wide, eventually affecting everything he was doing in his company, or rather, division, after Mitch bought them. "It put a strain on relationships everywhere and threw all of us into a totally reactive state. We became fearful. I even started reacting. It took me quite awhile to see what was happening to the division. I no longer felt I had any control. It was not a pretty picture and it didn't seem like there was much I could do to change it."

"If you happen to have charts on all this, Bill, I would like to see them."

"In fact I do, Mitch, but it would probably be better if you charted things yourself. I tried to convey all of this before, but like I said, I failed to communicate effectively. One of the things I've learned is that all of the steps to overcoming organizational blindness must be personally experienced in order to restore a leader's, or any other employee's, vision. We can do it together, if you'd like. Then you'll be able to tie it all back to the Assessment data and competencies."

"When do we start?"

"There is one more thing to talk about first, Mitch. It's called

creating context. Without it, we will just be doing another strategic planning exercise. I think you've done enough of them to realize that they don't produce real individual or organizational change."

CHAPTER 4 *Creating Context*

"**B**efore addressing these or any issues, I've found it is vital to create a powerful context for them. **Context** determines what we see. It's out of our context that we determine all meaning. It is all-defining."

"What do you mean by that?"

"It's really quite simple. But it's rather rare that anyone steps back to consciously define his or her context. Context is more than perspective. It is what determines your perspective. It is where you come from — and it determines the way you see everything around you. It determines all that exists in your personal world. I guess you could say that it's the source of what you think, see, hear and do. It's based on the way you hold, frame, or view things."

In explaining context, Bill likened it to a cup that holds water; that without the cup, you would not be able to drink or use its contents. "You see, Mitch, we're all just cups. As a cup, both of us — indeed all of us — determine the meaning we give to our lives. Context determines perspective. Perspective creates thoughts, and thoughts create experience. As a CEO, you determine what exists in your company. You are the cause. You are responsible. Think of it this way: You are a reservoir through which everything flows both in and out. And whatever passes through that reservoir is transformed."

ALL OF US DETERMINE THE MEANING

WE GIVE TO OUR LIVES.

Bill went on to explain that anytime you address organizational dilemmas or paradoxes without a consciously developed context, you unknowingly throw everything into a reactive state. You will only see events and surprises. And you will likely be consumed by fear.

Context is All Defining

RISING QUICKLY FROM HIS CHAIR, BILL TOOK A MARKER, and drew a black spot onto a sheet of flipchart paper. "What do you see, Mitch?"

•

"A black dot, of course. What else is there?"

"There is all of the space around it that makes the black dot possible. This is the context of the dot — the cup it lives in. Anytime you think you're addressing the spot you have taken it out of context and given it a life of its own. Once you have defined your personal context, it determines what you see. That's why I say context is all defining. The meaning you have given it is your own. That's how powerful context is."

Bill explained that if you have a context that believes in events as the cause of things you give a meaningless "dot" complete control over what you do. You give it meaning — and once you react to it — it has taken power over you. It takes control of what you think and do. It determines decisions, justifies actions and establishes ways of viewing reality. It now controls your destiny because it's how you choose to see the world. It's your world view. It becomes what you react to. It defines your entire executive decision making orientation. "Wow," Mitch sighed.

A MEANINGLESS "DOT" CAN TAKE CONTROL OF WHAT
YOU THINK AND DO. IT HAS ALL THE POWER. IT DETERMINES
DECISIONS, JUSTIFIES ACTIONS AND ESTABLISHES WAYS
OF VIEWING REALITY.

"Mitch, let me tell you a little story."

"Out here the ranges are so large it's not feasible to put gates everywhere a road crosses a fence in order to corral cattle. Plus none of the cowboys want to get off their horses or out of their trucks to open and close the gates. Since necessity is the mother of invention, some ranchers got together and invented the cattle guard — you've seen them — a ditch dug across the road with metal bars spanning the ditch every few inches.

"At first, cattle guards were a great success. Cows couldn't walk through them, and the cowboys could drive right over them. Then they discovered the downside. The driver, cargo and suspension of a pickup truck going over a cattle guard at sixty — even fifty miles an hour — takes a horrendous jolt.

"So once again some cowboys got together to tackle the problem. Someone suggested that since cows were not that bright, why not fill in the ditches and paint stripes across the dirt where the bars used to be?

And it worked. The painted lines kept the cows from straying. The cows would wander up to the painted cattle guards and automatically say to themselves, 'Hold it! That's a cattle guard; I can't go any further.'

"So the cows spent their days grazing in their assigned pasture, never questioning their fate. The cowboys, in their trucks or on horseback, no longer had to worry about the cattle guards. The painted bars kept the cattle in their assigned pastures."

"I think I understand," Mitch said with a crooked grin. "But I noticed when I was out West a few years ago that there were still cattle guards everywhere I went." Then he smiled, and they both laughed.

"That's true, and that's the rest of the story. One day, a couple of cowboys found a herd that had crossed a painted cattle guard to graze in the rich grass close to the North Platt River.

"It appeared that one curious cow went up to the painted cattle guard and really examined it. There was something odd about it. So she cautiously put one hoof on the cattle guard and it didn't fall through. Examining the lines very carefully, she realized they were not real. They were just paint. 'Paint!' she thought. 'All this time we've been fenced in by a pretend cattle guard!' The possibility that this wasn't a real cattle guard went against the herd mind set. They all thought that cattle guards were impassible barriers. That's just the way things were!

"Faced with the consequences of being fenced in by paint, the cow summoned all her courage. And although she was terrified, she put another hoof on a painted line. Still nothing happened. Then, she took a deep breath and triumphantly walked across. Only then did she confirm that the cattle guard — which had kept her fenced in for so long — was just made up!"

"That sounds like me crossing the swinging bridge this morning," Mitch said with a reflective smile.

"So she immediately went back and led the entire herd across the painted cattle guard and into the richer pastures."

"Great story, Bill."

Returning to his seat at the conference table, Bill put his little story into an organizational context. "Calling things problems sets up a context that defines our job as problem solvers. Much like the cowboys out on the range, that's what most managers think their job is — to solve problems. Some think all they do is fight fires. Further, they often have a belief that if there are 100 fires, there must be 100 solutions. It makes the fires bigger and management smaller. Problems suddenly take on a life of their own — they take control — ."

" — Just like the painted cattle guards," Mitch said, finishing Bill's thought. "So first we need to examine what's fencing us in; most often we'll discover that the barriers are simply made up, just like the paint that kept the cows in."

"Here's what I've found, Mitch, that aims directly at the heart of going from a reactive state to creating a Generative Organization and inspired performance. You need a consciously developed context based on fundamental choices and principles. That is what will allow you to determine and control your future.

What You See is a Reflection of Where You Come From

"REMEMBER, YOUR CONTEXT DETERMINES WHAT YOU SEE and the meaning of everything that happens to you and around you. For example, when you focus on serving others, you see them serving you. In this context you see others as your mirror. Conversely, if you are self-serving you will just see others serving themselves or even trying to take advantage of you. What you see in them is a reflection of who you are."

"REMEMBER, YOUR CONTEXT DETERMINES WHAT YOU SEE AND THE MEANING OF EVERYTHING THAT HAPPENS TO YOU AND AROUND YOU."

Mitch acknowledged that two people walking into the same room will see the same identical situation in a totally different way, based on their past experiences. And he admitted that leaders who are full of fear will likely cause fear in others. He related the fear many of his associates had within GT during his years there.

"To be able to effectively manage yourself — or lead others — requires mastery," Bill reinforced, "or at the very least a concrete understanding of context. Context is your frame of reference — but much more powerful. It is frame of reference times ten, because it determines and justifies all of your decisions and actions."

CHAPTER 5 *The Generative Context*

"The context for achieving inspired performance," Bill reiterated, "is a Generative Context. It's based on the three insights about energy that we talked about on the phone the other night."

"I wrote them down and thought a great deal about them on the flight out here." After a pause, Mitch continued, "Bill, I want you to know that I believe I came here for a very special purpose. While I was completing the assessment, I became very reflective about where we are along our pathway. By the way, I had all my managers read *Good to Great*. I told them this is where we are headed. But your assessment really laid out a road map to get there that the book did not.

"I am slowly beginning to grasp how profound, yet simple, it all is. My energy is different, and as we talk I'm actually letting in what you have to say. Normally, I would probably just analyze, evaluate and judge it. I am sure that's how I defend myself from change. I see that now. A few evenings ago, I realized how arrogant I was to think I had the answers to everything, or that I could control things."

Bill nodded in understanding and reflected, "About all we can do is let others in — or keep them out. I can tell that you're open and willing to change your context. But out here in the wide-open spaces, new ideas come in more easily than they do in a corporate environment. Really, Mitch, all that a generative context boils down to is the three insights I shared with you, a few core principles, making fundamental choices, and following the laws of nature. They operate all of the time — with or without our permission or knowledge. That's the bottom line.

"ABOUT ALL WE CAN DO IS LET OTHERS IN—

OR KEEP THEM OUT."

"The other thing that's important to grasp right now is that the only person you can change is yourself. And when you change, the whole world is changed." Mitch shook his head in acknowledgment.

After some silence, Bill continued. "It's the place you come from that allows you to be a contributive force in the world. Once you have this context, all you will see are principles either being followed or violated. To live by these principles takes discipline and discipleship, yet to violate them causes suffering for both you and others. These principles and laws are based on the way the world works. They are nothing I discovered or invented. They have always existed — and will continue to exist — forever."

". . . THE ONLY PERSON YOU CAN CHANGE IS YOURSELF;
WHEN YOU CHANGE, THE WHOLE WORLD IS CHANGED."

The Forces of Nature Always Win
BILL WENT ON TO EXPRESS THE WISDOM HE HAD GAINED from working with the tribal council, which espoused an alignment with the forces of nature. "The forces of nature, they say, will always win. The alternative is to be at the effect of your own human nature. Either way, it is your context that acts as the lens through which you see things. This determines the choices you make, and therefore, the way you behave. Unless you clearly see where you are coming from and consciously build your context — you will be at the mercy of everything around you. You will be stuck in a reactive state.

Seeing Yourself as a Projector and the World as Your Screen
"WHEN YOU REALLY MASTER CONTEXT," Bill continued, "you will see yourself as a projector that takes whatever is inside of you, how you think about things, and projects it onto your world. That's how you know who you are — by an honest assessment of what you project onto others."

Each Moment Lasts Forever
WALKING TO THE WINDOW OVERLOOKING THE RESERVATION, Bill told Mitch that the shaman serving the council believes that each moment is eternity, and that when you take a **pause-a-tive** view, you can see forever. Pausing allows you to see the future — kind of like a preview — before you project yourself onto the world around you. "It is better, he says, to

stop and preview everything before you say it; in other words, proofread it before you send it. That way you can see if you are working with the Forces of Nature or projecting your own agenda based on your self-serving human nature."

"So," Mitch said, "all I actually see is just a projection of who I am and where I come from." He shook his head, displaying a rueful smile. "I think

I'm getting all this, but it's a bit abstract for me. I know if we were to have this kind of discussion while addressing our problems at work, people wouldn't be very understanding or take the time to really consider it. You know how I like things concrete and logical. I've always trusted the numbers — and certainly been bottom line oriented. I am not a great relationship person. Everywhere I look I see numbers and measurements. I guess that's my context…and it does cause a reactive state. That's for sure. Ironically, I do love philosophy."

"Mitch, you have just nailed the greatest challenge I have in working with CEOs, even those who show up truly committed to inspired performance.

"Here's my take on that. What you create, or don't create for yourself shows up in all those you influence. As a CEO, and even as a front line supervisor, you, or any person, may not have any real control over things. But still, you influence and activate emotions inside of everyone."

Bill put forth the example that if your context is 'What's in it for me?' that will determine what you see. He explained that it also causes others to look out for themselves. He emphasized how fear drives everything, causing people to come from scarcity. "You will always project onto others what is actually within your self. That is all you can see. Then everyone around you becomes fearful."

Victims are Blamers

"ANOTHER EXAMPLE CAN BE SEEN IN PEOPLE WHO BLAME OTHERS. People who blame others are playing a victim role in the organization. The position of 'I am a victim of others' will also determine what you see. It results in others being responsible for whatever happens. It is never your fault."

Coming back to the table, Bill continued, "Mastering context is the only thing that allows me to maintain a generative, as opposed to reactive, orientation. It's what helps me keep things, as you used to say in board meetings, in 'perspective.'"

Seating himself next to Mitch, Bill paused a moment before continuing. "Here's something that may surprise you. When I feel things are out of my control I get fearful, and there is nothing I can do about it. I started having panic attacks when things were not going well in the company. I would wake up nights thinking about things I could not control or was afraid of losing. It was the fear of failing and of losing everything that I had built. My self-image was attached to the company. That's one reason I had to leave your management team, Mitch. I had to understand why I was so afraid of losing control….why I was afraid of letting go."

"YOU WILL ALWAYS PROJECT ONTO OTHERS WHAT IS ACTUALLY WITHIN YOURSELF. THAT IS ALL YOU CAN SEE. THEN EVERYONE AROUND YOU BECOMES FEARFUL."

Startled to hear Bill's confession, Mitch, too, felt very vulnerable. He knew Bill was inviting him into his inner self by sharing his fear of being out of control. He felt very close to Bill, in a way he could not remember feeling with any of his work associates before.

During a period of thoughtful silence, Mitch walked over to the large picture window surrounding them and soaked in the vista before him. "You know, Bill, I thought that having my Wharton MBA, being one of the youngest managers of a GT division and then actually running the GT leadership academy for two years had prepared me for running my own business. It's certainly what convinced my investors to put up the money. They believed I could create a competitive advantage by implementing my acquisition growth strategy."

Turning back to face Bill, Mitch continued, "I realize now that I didn't have a clue, nor did they. Actually, it caused me to be overly confident and unable to see what was going on around me, even though I thought I was on top of everything. Up here, in this place, I am able to not only hear, but also really see what I have been doing that has limited our growth. It is happening as we talk. Thanks for sharing with me; I have been experiencing very similar emotions and anxieties. I never called them panic attacks, but I guess in a way they are.

"The very idea that successfully running a business has anything to do with being able to create a context for myself had never crossed my mind.

But the truth is, that's what has gotten me as far as I've been able to go. I completely agree with the idea that my way of viewing reality is what determines what I see. Yet all I seem to see are the problems or situations that cause us to be reactive."

As he moved back to the conference table, Mitch admitted, "What I didn't realize is what I couldn't see due to my own blindness. I virtually considered anything that someone said that countered my way of doing things as negative. Of course I didn't tell them that. Actually what I did was openly encourage other opinions and ideas. But at the same time, I cut off all kinds of resources. I even cut you off. I am sure that I also influenced how others behaved around me and limited the contributions they made. I certainly was the cause of your anxieties. I can see that."

"When we meet in the tribal councils, we go through a ritual of cleansing ourselves of self-serving thoughts. It's our way of addressing the forces that make up our self-image. They limit our vision and capacity for contribution. You can't focus on your personal dream or vision and look out for your self at the same time. They are mutually exclusive. Self-serving thoughts cause fear in others because they are rooted in a circle of fear. A circle of fear called self-image."

The Self Image

"What's this got to do with self-image, Bill? I'm not sure I understand what you're talking about. Earlier you mentioned that your self-image was attached to your company. I didn't quite understand what you meant."

Bill replied, "Well one way to understand it is to simply think about who you think you are. Let's call it your concept of 'self' or 'me'."

"You mean ego — that kind of stuff?"

"Absolutely. If I were to draw a circle on the paper here and label it ME, what would be inside of the circle called me and what would be on the outside?"

"That's easy enough. Inside are all of my roles, thoughts, beliefs, opinions, values, emotions — who I think I am. Outside is everything else. My family…others… things I own… the weather…my business…suppliers…the bankers who won't loan me money right now." They both laughed. "Basically, the things that seem to upset me, even those things that give me pleasure, seem to be outside of me. Is that what you mean?"

"Absolutely, Mitch. Play along with me here for a moment. How would you define the word 'image'?"

"Well, it's a reflection…an imitation. It's probably based on the root of the word, so it is something that is imagined…or something that is not real."

"Yes, and if you go a step further in the dictionary, it would say it is something that does not exist. You could say it's just made up. So if we believe we are our self-image, and it's just made up, nothing we see is real either."

"So that's why everyone is so easily threatened," Mitch offered. "They're always protecting and defending something that's not real. Is that what you mean by a circle of fear?" Bill nodded affirmatively.

"So let me see if I've got this straight. If we are projectors of our self-image (that actually doesn't exist) but we think is real, what we see is not real either . . . even though we think it is . . . and what we are projecting is our fears and other stuff we make up. Is that about it?" Both men smiled.

Who Are We?

"SO THE NEXT LOGICAL QUESTION I HAVE IS, 'IF WE AREN'T OUR SELF-IMAGE, who are we?' And a far less significant question, but one that's on my mind right now, is 'what does all this have to do with creating inspired performance? What does this have to do with my trip out here?' Bill, all of a sudden I feel really frustrated and confused by all of this. Even though I am enjoying this discussion, I think we may be wasting precious time on such abstract ideas."

"Well, Mitch, it does get a bit tricky at this point, but it explains a few things that could be of value. For instance," he elaborated, turning back to the flip chart, "number one is why we tend to be so reactive to events or to the things that we believe are outside of us, and number two, why we are only generative when coming from a context based on principles, fundamental choices — and, of course, the laws of nature.

"But to answer your question, 'if we aren't our self-image, who are we?' requires a far more personal answer. For me, all I am is the context I'm able to create for myself, my vision or dream for the future…and even more fundamentally…the principles I choose to live by. That's about it. I guess everyone has to answer that question at some point in their life. If not, what you are not will eventually consume you."

Mitch did not say anything.

After a while Bill stood up. "I'm going to the sweat lodge now. It's down the path behind the lodge. You can join me if you'd like. There's a robe in your room, which is at the top of the stairs and to the right, beside the library. In the library, I left a small book with some thoughts you may find helpful. I usually refer to it when I'm faced with major considerations. I often reread it before I go to the sweat lodge.

"Mitch, keep in mind that leaders who are committed to implementing the kind of change within their organizations that results in aligning people and releasing energy for inspired performance need to see themselves as servants. And, to serve, first they must be change agents.

Anyway, in the little book you'll find some of my thoughts as I was learning to master context. You may find some value in them as well."

CHAPTER 6 *Mastering Context*

Mitch walked outside with his head spinning. This was not at all what he had expected. He ran some of the most intensive training programs that GT ever produced, including the famous 'workout program' and was charged with the original launch of Six Sigma. Nothing had prepared him for the past several hours with Bill or the crossing of the chasm. Yet he was able to admit that his way of viewing reality had begun to shift. What would it all mean? Better yet, what would it take to be generative and create inspired performance? "When I am reactive, do I project my way of thinking onto things? Is everything around me just a screen of what I am projecting? Have I been defending a self-image that doesn't really exist?"

This was not just about leadership or management training any longer, he realized. It was reaching inside to discover an entirely new way of looking at things. A new orientation. In the back of his mind, Mitch suspected that Bill was just laying the groundwork for what was yet to come. "Am I up for this?" he pondered.

As he walked around to the front of the lodge, Mitch's mind was a jumble of conflicting thoughts. "A part of me really wants to hold onto what has gotten me this far. Clearly I have been successful by all standards in my business career. Granted, my personal life has had its problems. The divorce was painful to the kids and ended up in bitterness," he admitted. "But now that I'm moving on in that area of my life — the company is all of a sudden in jeopardy." Could all of this have been going on and he just could not see it? What if the money crisis had not hit? Would he have even taken notice or made the trip out to Wyoming? "I think not," he said conclusively.

"Then there's the experience with SynergyCorp that I can't get out of my mind. They literally saved the day. They were actually grateful to repay Bill for his contribution to them. Most amazing of all — they were just suppliers of his, not customers, suppliers. Something special is going on here and I want to be a part of it. It is different than anything I have ever known in the world of business. There's a real challenge before me and I'm not sure the person who got off the plane outside Thermopolis will be returning home. I'm somehow different already. It's not a skill or technique that I'm learning, it's an orientation. It's about how I view the world. It's about who I am."

After some time soaking in the view and reflecting on the day, Mitch decided to take what he anticipated would be a step into a brave new world. He came in and went to his room at the top of the stairs. He changed into his robe and headed to the sweat lodge. "What will this be all about?" he wondered a bit anxiously.

As he passed the library and glanced in, something about it spoke to him. He spotted the book that was placed on a coffee table made from a beautifully preserved cross-section of a tree. Based on the number of growth rings, it was clearly hundreds of years old. As he entered the library, he felt drawn to discover what Bill had found meaningful enough to write about, reread and reflect upon.

Opening the book and starting to read, Mitch suddenly felt vulnerable. He eased himself into the large leather chair beside the desk.

Mastering Context

FIRST AND FOREMOST, PLEASE REMEMBER THAT YOU AREN'T YOUR POSITION or title or even whoever you think you are. The only thing that you are or will ever be (or have) is what you contribute. You will always (and only) receive that which you give to others. Be mindful of what you give — it is who you are.

Free yourself of your perceptions, beliefs, judgments, thoughts, influences, experiences and illusions that are not based on fundamental truths and principles. Be free from who you are not. Be honest about your image of yourself. It is just imagined. It is not real.

You are not what your mind perceives, but always remember that that is all most people know of themselves or others. That is why we all see things so differently. Rather, know you are only the spirit that is deep within you, when connected to God. Prepare yourself daily to receive this spirit. When you do, you will see and respect it within everyone and every thing.

The tribal council teaches that life presents many powerful endurances. They act like an internal guidance system. They provide the source of sustained growth

Of these endurances, self-awareness, reflection and self-management are

self-awareness that leads to self-management you are doomed to reacting to events. You will be the victim of your own misperceptions and at the effect of the illusions of others. When you are the cause and are responsible, then you are free. Freedom only comes from being responsible. The only alternative to freedom is being a victim.

Self-awareness begins with being and seeing everything as connected. All energy in life comes from you being connected and fully using the powers gifted you by God, as the creator of all things. As you increase your relationship and connectedness with God, greater energy flows through you, both to and from others. You are a vessel through which energy is released or suppressed. God uses this vessel for His purpose. Follow His will, not your own.

FREE YOURSELF OF YOUR PERCEPTIONS, BELIEFS, JUDGMENTS, THOUGHTS, INFLUENCES, EXPERIENCES AND ILLUSIONS THAT ARE NOT BASED ON FUNDAMENTAL TRUTHS AND PRINCIPLES.

Wisdom comes from discovering the truth about each experience. Truth has no beginning or ending. It is eternal. Whether you see it or you miss it, it is all that exists. You can't see it when you are consumed with your own self interests and have not forgiven others or are unforgiving of yourself. Understand that the way things are now is how they are forever. Live this moment fully. It is forever.

Nature was created perfectly. All things (including organizations) work perfectly as they were designed. Nature is truthful. It will never deceive you if you listen. The way of freedom (and nature) requires that you direct your life toward your purpose on this earth. When you are off purpose, you — and others in your life — will suffer. Your purpose is the reason for which you exist. It is why you are on this dirt. Be not deceived by the mis / perceptions formed by the imprints on your disk of life. They will let you down. They are beliefs, perceptions and judgments. They will deceive you. They will not serve you or your life's purpose. Rely on principles and laws and seek to know the truth in all things.

The present is yours for eternity. The present is a gift, that is why it is called "present." It will always be there. This reality is the driving motivation for all real _hange. If you believe in eternity, it is all there is or can be. Therefore, because this eternity will last forever, make it your grandest and most magnificent moment.

If you do not believe in eternity, eat, drink and be merry. Get as much from life as you can, but understand that life will be a struggle with no real satisfaction. You will be a taker — not one who gives.

However, if you do believe in eternity, the way things are now is the way they will always be. What is not forgiven will prevent you from giving. It will never heal and will remain with you. To forgive....is to give as before.

Begin each moment with gratitude and forgiveness. What you do not forgive will hold you as its prisoner. You will be controlled by your judgments, beliefs and perceptions. What you hold onto, you will not have. It will have you. Let go. Release yourself from your beliefs, perceptions and judgments. They aren't real anyway.

The Six Powers

YOU POSSESS SIX POWERS, WHICH INCREASE YOUR CONNECTEDNESS and allow energy to flow through you. The sole purpose of the six powers is for you to transcend the illusion of your own reactive state and separateness. When you are on purpose, you will be connected and generative. When you are off-purpose you will disconnect from yourself and others. When you are disconnected, you become who you are not. You become alone and afraid. You become reactive.

In order to use the six powers you must be open to ridding yourself of all forms of blindness, deafness, numbness and prejudices. Always know that there are influences and influencers that have made imprints on your disk of life and distort your ability to see and hear. Also, be aware that each power has its inverse influence. Misused or not understood, any of these powers can destroy and take away life.

The Power of Giving

SURRENDER TO THE POWER OF GIVING. Giving endures through all time. Giving is like the 'life giving power of water.' What you give is all you will ever have. It determines all you will receive. It is the sole source of any joy.

Even the power of giving has the power to destroy...to take away from life. Give carefully. Your choice of what you give will influence everything that is available to you from the remaining powers. Surrender and give. Give up what ever you are holding on to that keeps you from surrendering.

80

The Power of Forgiveness, Gratefulness and Healing

THE POWER OF FORGIVENESS IS THE SOURCE OF ALL THAT HEALS. *Healing comes from forgiveness.*

Forgiveness releases energy and gives you the gift of grace. Grace is only possible when you are grateful. Gratefulness brings you peace and opens you up to the knowledge that comes from surrendering to the truth. When you forgive, you release yourself from the misperceptions that come from thinking about your self. Thinking about your own self interests causes separateness and suffering. Self-knowledge starts with seeing yourself and all things as connected. It represents the soil into which seeds are planted for the development of wisdom.

The Power of Completeness, Surrender and Service

COMPLETENESS IS ESSENTIAL FOR CLEANSING, REST, ENDURANCE AND THE RESTORATION OF STRENGTH. What is incomplete has not fulfilled its purpose and will stay with you until it is complete. When it is complete, it is over, and you will be emptied. Be willing to be left empty. Be willing to not know . . . . but be complete. What is incomplete will not allow you to create anew. You must be willing to let go of what you hold onto to live fully and be able to serve others… without holding back. It is from this state of surrender that you can lead…. so that you can fulfill a mighty purpose worthy of your life during your time on this earth. Only when you are serving are you living fully, as you were intended to do.

The Power of Rebirth

THE POWER OF REBIRTH LEADS TO ABUNDANCE. Rebirth is the source of all true growth. Rebirth exists when you are giving to and serving others. Where you come from is either a state of abundance or scarcity. Who you are is reborn each time you serve others and give yourself away. Who you are not is your self-serving human nature. The way of nature is giving. Do not confuse giving with getting.

The Power of Vision

TO LEAD YOU MUST SEE OVER TIME, SPACE AND CAUSALITY. When you lack vision, you will only see what affects your own self-interests. You will not see beyond your own perceptions of yourself. If you do not see over time, space and causality you will react to what is not real. Vision is the very source of the river of communication between *yourself and others. It allows you to connect with the true nature of others.*

The Power of Stewardship

YOU ARE THE STEWARD OF YOUR ORGANIZATION.When you respect "the spirit of your people" you release their energy to contribute. When you release the spirit of others, you release your own spirit. Inspired performance is possible only when you have complete respect for others and yourself. You are here to be your organization's steward.What you fail to attend to or leave incomplete will consume you. Complete everything.

You have dominion over all things.
Use these powers wisely.

Mitch rose and returned the book to its place on the table. Then, in a bit of a daze, he descended the stairs and walked outside to the path leading to the sweat lodge. What did all that mean? 'Who I am is only what I contribute.' 'What I have is what I give away to others.' 'Complete everything.' 'I have dominion over all things.'

The sweat lodge was covered with a form of grass or sod and seemed to be built into the side of the mountain. He opened the door and once inside could not see anything due to the thick steam and humidity. It was somewhat like the steam room at his club, but the surrounding warmth was very calming, like a heavy blanket. There were bearskin rugs on the earthen floor. He could not see anyone else in the room. He sat down and quickly felt his pores opening up. Sweat began to drench his robe. The tension seemed to fade away, as did his thought process.

The door opened and he could see the shape of the cowboy, his guide, coming in with a bucket of water. As he poured it on the rocks in the middle of the lodge, steam consumed the room and the cowboy's image faded as though he were never there.

"Mr. Crandall, just listen to your breathing," he said. Then silence.

In the silence, Mitch began to focus on his breathing as he was instructed. He could hear his heart pounding, sounding like thunder in the night. The sound was so loud that it was like an explosion in his head. He felt like he was sitting outside his body, watching intently. Then, the six powers from the book started to shape his way of thinking and his thoughts about himself.

Suddenly Mitch was flooded with memories. He could see what he had done to succeed. The pattern was the same: from grade school to high school, through college, and in his career. "It was always about me," he thought. "Trying to get ahead, to accomplish. Trying to achieve goals and objectives. That's what I was always about. When I was given divisions to turn around....when I headed up the United Way. I thought it was to contribute — yet now I can see it was to gain recognition. What have I done that was truly giving?" Mitch realized how driven he'd been his whole life. "But by what?" he asked himself. "Was it all fear?"

Then Mitch started seeing the people in his life pass before him. He pictured Charlotte, his childhood sweetheart. "We went all the way through high school and college together, and then we married. But we never really knew each other."

He thought of his two boys, Mark and John, and how they were so different. "Mark," he thought, "is just like me. He's following in my footsteps." Then Mitch had to admit some harsh realities to himself. "Even though Mark works in the company, we aren't that close. We never really share. Not really...not about ourselves. Of course we talk about the company and what he needs to do next to develop and hone his skills."

Then he pictured John, who had really struggled — never quite fitting into the family. As he thought about John's problem with drugs, Mitch realized for the first time that he was ashamed of his response: forming an anti-drug campaign in all the schools. "It tore me up the time John said he 'wished I was not his father.' Why couldn't I have just spent time with him?" he agonized.

"John my boy, I am so sorry," he said out loud, as tears welled up inside him and for the first time ever, turned into uncontrollable sobs.

After awhile, Mitch's mind returned to Charlotte, and how much they were alike. They were both achievers. But she had taken the time for the kids that he never did, even though Charlotte was in charge of the symphony fundraiser for their new building and sat on several committees with the Governor of Georgia. "She's been a great mother," he acknowledged.

"Now she's been invited to go to Washington if the Governor gets elected President. Wow."

It was painful to acknowledge that it took several years after the divorce for them to talk about what went wrong in their marriage. They both cried at the time, realizing how much they had missed, even though they both had more than they'd ever dreamed of financially, plus a lot of influence within the community.

Mitch also realized that the only time he had ever felt real intimacy with anyone was one time with his father, an immigrant to whom nothing came easily. The experience only lasted a few minutes when his father was on his deathbed, but they both told each other how much they loved one another. "He told me how sorry he was for pushing me so hard. He felt he had to be tough to raise me to succeed in this world. Then he said how sorry he was to realize that we had never been close — even though we went hunting together and he was my baseball coach and was involved in parent programs. That was the only time I felt completely whole." Sitting there in the sweat lodge, tears flowed down Mitch's cheeks as he realized that he had done the same thing to his sons.

Then Mitch thought about his old CEO who told him, after a long weekend of working together on a project that having "all of this" meant nothing to him. "It is only a game," Mitch recalled him saying. "What life is about is fulfilling your purpose. It's doing what God put you on this earth to do. It's about relationships...first with God...then with yourself...and finally with others."

"Funny how I didn't let that piece of advice in back then," Mitch reflected, "but at this moment, I'm consumed by it. . . How unreal. It's been twelve years since I heard or thought about those comments. But that's all we really have. And I've never focused on developing real relationships, especially in that order."

Mitch felt toxins and hurts from a lifetime of striving coming forth from him to experience. At times he felt like he was looking at his entire life from above, yet experiencing every moment of it as though he was deeply rooted in the earth. Very slowly he felt a pervasive calmness throughout his body. Everything seemed complete, yet he had done nothing at all to achieve this feeling. He felt forgiveness and gratefulness and finally, peace. He felt drained, but totally energized to share with others. He let go, yet he felt connected to everyone. Most importantly he felt alive, like he was generating new energy to give to others.

When Mitch got up and opened the door to the sweat lodge, the sun had gone down. It was a cool, crisp evening. He realized that he must have been there for hours. Some lanterns were lit along the path. The moon and stars were absolutely brilliant. He felt like he could reach out and touch them . . . like they were shining directly upon him.

When Mitch entered Bill's lodge, the lights were dim and no one was up, but there was a note on the counter: *I left some food in the oven for you. If you're cold, just put a small log in the wood burning stove and give it about 10 minutes to heat up. Enjoy. See you in the morning. Bill.*

Mitch was absolutely starving, and the stew was incredible. The bread was so chocked full of grains that there was a new taste in every bite. His mind was completely empty. Just gratitude remained . . . peace.

CHAPTER *7 The Generate Vision*

The next day Mitch could both hear and smell the coffee percolating in the kitchen downstairs. Bread was baking and it was a glorious aroma, like going into a bakery early in the morning. "This is great," he thought to himself. His energy was fully recovered from the previous day, and he could breathe deeply without any restriction. There was none of the familiar rush or pressure that he had been feeling in his chest for the past several months. He felt free of all tension and stress. His self-concerns were gone. He could see from an exhilarating and different place.

As he came down the stairs, the cowboy, who seemed to appear from nowhere, began silently going about his business of preparing breakfast. "How do you want your eggs, Mr. Crandall? They're fresh from the hen house this morning. I think you will find them quite special."

"However you like them yourself, thanks." Mitch realized that he did not know the cowboy's name, nor had he offered it. He decided to leave it that way.

Bill came in from outside. "How are you, Mitch? I just got back from a great hike. Perhaps you can join me tomorrow. There is so much for you to see while you're out here. You were sleeping so soundly, I didn't want to disturb you."

"What time is it?"

"It's about one in the afternoon," Bill said.

Mitch realized he had slept for 12 hours solid. Normally he woke up at four or five a.m. and worked while it was quiet. This had never happened before that he could remember, except after pulling an all-nighter during final exam week in college.

You Can Only Let Others In

MITCH WAS APPRECIATIVE THAT BILL REFRAINED from asking about his evening in the sweat lodge or what his experience was like. He still had not sorted it out himself. He just knew that somehow he would never be the same. He now had a perspective that he could not see before. Instead of looking at people and trying to control or analyze them — he realized that all he could *ever* do was let them in. What was important before, seemed to have little or no value at all; what was previously not recognized as having any importance seemed to be all that mattered now.

When Mitch had finished eating, Bill suggested they pick up from where they left off yesterday so they could talk some real business strategy. "Then we can do some planning on Monday before you leave."

Seated back at the conference table Mitch said, "You know Bill, what I most want is to capture in our company is what SynergyCorp brought to us on Thursday and Friday when they delivered our parts. What they really brought to us was their spirit. It had a very profound impact on me and all of our people. That's clearly what matters to me now. If we have that, we will fulfill all our dreams and my vision for the company.

"We have always had a vision statement, but not vision. I never knew there was a difference. Now I know that's what I came here for. I think that's what you had in your company before we dismantled it after you left. It would be incredible if we could show up to serve our customers in that manner, and have the impact you had on your suppliers that caused them to serve us as they did."

When You Serve You See Everything Serving You
"Mitch, you are seeing things from a very powerful context right now. When you lead by serving others, you will see everyone around you serving you. At the moment of serving, everything becomes a resource to achieving your dream.

"Now let's take the steps to seeing generatively or restoring your vision. That's another way for us to address overcoming organizational blindness."

Five Levels of Seeing
Moving to the flipchart, Bill continued, "Generative Vision is a developmental process that has five levels to it.

Today's Solutions become Tomorrow's Problems
"On the **first level**, you will simply see that today's solutions become

tomorrow's problems. You will begin to notice that there are no real solutions, and realize that, over time, there are actually no problems. This is certainly no easy task, because what gets our attention tends to be events, surprises and problems. So this is often all we notice. It is all we can see. It's our human nature. It's the reactive orientation.

"On the **second level**, a problem or event — when defined dynamically over time — becomes a pattern of behavior. Patterns can only be seen over time.

"On the **third level**, you will be able to see the principles and fundamental choices that determine the patterns, including the underlying structures that cause behavior.

"And on the **fourth level**, you will be able to see the leverage points (around which you align the organization) that remove the source of upset conditions and limits to growth. You will be the source of implementing strategies of optimum growth that are designed to maintain organizational balance and sustain a generative state.

"A final **fifth level** is seeing that the way you and your team think is the underlying structure of the organization. You are the designers."

When Bill had finished, the five levels of organizational vision — or seeing generatively, as he called it — were clearly outlined. Although Mitch had never had this perspective of his organization, he could see that the actual cause of his difficulties came from the violation of principles and reacting to events. He had been organizationally blind and now could see.

5. See yourself as the designer of the organization

4. See leverage points; align the organization around them

3. See underlying structure (causality) made up of control feedback loops

2. See patterns and trends that are increasing and decreasing over time—recognize there are no problems or events

1. See what others see that causes a reactive state to exist: recurring events, problems, quick fixes, long term consequences

"Bill, it seems to me that you are sliding into teaching one of the seminars I used to run at the GT Leadership Academy, only now I'm the one taking notes. I don't mind telling you that even though I taught all of that stuff and had a hand in developing the curriculum, very few of our executives actually implemented it afterward. Why that is, I am not sure. In fact, I'm not sure how much, if any of it, I have used now that I am running my own show. I still preach it though. I was brutally honest when I filled out the organizational assessment. I approached each question by assessing what we had actually implemented versus what we had just started or put on hold. It was very revealing."

"Probably Mitch, the simple answer is that executives get right back into reacting to events — and the learning is quickly dissipated. I don't need to tell you that when events happen it's almost impossible to give your attention to the right things, especially for the right amount of time, till you get the desired result.

"However, the more deeply rooted (and more subtle) answer seems to lie in the way most organizations are wired up — they are designed to react to the past — not create the future. For instance, financials tend to drive a huge amount of behavior. Think how, in a public company, the quarterly earnings report can drive all kinds of reactive behavior, including expense freezes or shelving major initiatives. Sometimes they will go on all-out campaigns to drive revenue to meet Wall Street's expectations for short-term earnings reports, with little or no concern about other consequences or long term profit. In a privately held organization like yours, it can be pressure from bankers or Venture Capital groups, or just the need for cash to fund other initiatives. Most often, it's all a reaction to competition."

"Certainly, a great deal of financial pressure for us has been driven by our growth strategy. Acquisitions have consumed us. We consider them major events. But getting the parts this last week and orders out the door — as small and routine as that seems — became major."

After being lost in thought for a moment, Mitch continued. "Bill, if you don't mind, give me a real example of patterns of behavior over time and how structure causes behavior. I think I know where you're headed when talking about how organizations are wired up and are reactive, but a real-world explanation would help in approaching my situation."

"Sure, Mitch. Think for a moment how water flows according to the shape of the land. Water first fills various openings or crevices. It goes to the lowest possible level available. Then when the crevices are filled it moves on. Assuming the level of water is rising, it's totally guided by the contour of the land. But no matter what, water always takes the path of least resistance."

"So, the pattern of behavior is the water, and the land is the structure."

"Exactly!"

"So what would a pattern of behavior be like in an organization?" Mitch persisted.

"I'll share the story of one of my clients. Some time back I did a lot of work in the headquarters and plants of a good-sized company that makes paper products, plywood and OSB board. I was sent to see what I could do with their worst-performing plant. When I showed up, during our first plant management meeting, I asked them what dominated their time. One of the managers who had been there 30 years said, 'We fight fires.' I responded, "Oh, like they do at your corporate headquarters in Atlanta?" He said, 'No. We fight real fires!' He proceeded to take out a match and light it on the bottom of his boot — something I have never been able to do, by the way.

"So I responded, 'Who plans, organizes, schedules and benefits from these fires? Who gets a bonus when they happen?' They looked at me like I was crazy. 'They just happen,' the manager said. 'Like the bumper sticker on the back of cars that says S— Happens.' Everyone in the room agreed. Some actually smiled.

"I said, 'If you don't mind then, let's take a look at your fire fighting. Do you have downtime charts based on fires?'

'No — why would we?' he responded with a bit of agitation. 'They just happen!'

"Do you have downtime charts at all?" I inquired. They said, 'Of course – we chart and document everything here. We're ISO certified,' they said proudly. I said, 'Fine – let's look at them together.' We took a break while they gathered the downtime charts.

"After we reconvened and did about an hour of analysis, we had plotted out all of the downtime caused by fires in their plant. Here's what we discovered."

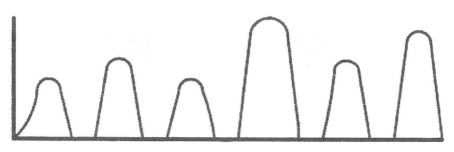

Downtime caused by fires over a period of time.

"What do you notice, Mitch?"

"I see a pattern — it just keeps repeating itself."

"What else do you notice?"

"It's repetitive and consistent–consistent over time."

"That's exactly what I saw as well. Then I took a real risk, betting my entire credibility with them, and said, 'Best I can tell — you are going to have one today, or at least before I leave — with a little variance due to leap year.' (I added that to inject some humor into my prediction. This time there were no smiles.)

"At three o'clock — by Divine Intervention I believe — the fire alarm went off. Everyone was out the door, throwing on yellow fire coats and hats and heading for the fire. They knew exactly what their roles were. They were great fire fighters, just like he said. It took us close to an hour and a half to extinguish the flames. I was right out there — getting wet and sooty with the best of them."

Mitch laughed appreciatively.

"The point is this: What they thought was an event that 'just happened' was a pattern of behavior over time. It was clearly a recurring pattern — and they had been 'solving' this problem for over 25 years. They had done all kinds of things to address putting the fires out more efficiently. Ironically, they had designed and developed four levels of independently sourced sprinkler systems that had been installed throughout the plant. Their approach was so successful that the other plants in the division brought them in to show how they did it and share their engineering drawings. They had a lot of pride in their way of fighting fires."

"That's a great illustration. How did it turn out? But more importantly — I guess the real question is, what was the underlying structure that caused the pattern of fires to occur? Is that the right question? And, are they still having fires? That's the major issue, isn't it?"

"Mitch, the last I heard they hadn't had a fire since we worked together. It's been eleven years with neither a fire nor any lost-time accidents taking place."

"You mean lost-time accidents could be charted as well?"

"Not only were they easily charted, but we found a very significant recurring pattern. They were totally predictable. Just like their fires."

"How many patterns were you able to chart?'

"By the end of our first three days together we had identified over forty patterns of 'upset conditions' that led to some form of significant reactive behavior. These were in addition to the first chart done on down time caused by fires."

"So what was the cause? Wait, let me answer my own question, Bill. It was the shape of the land. So the organization was actually designed to cause fires – not just the real fires, but their patterns of reactive behavior. How did they redesign the organization that resulted in no fires or lost time accidents? What other upset conditions were they able to eliminate? Is there a step-by-step method for doing this that we can also follow?"

"There wasn't then, Mitch, but there is now. It's still quite iterative, however. I did the original work with them some time before starting the company you bought from me. When I started my own company, I wanted to learn how to integrate all the principles from the perspective of the business owner and management team. Believe me, doing it myself on a day to day basis was quite different from coming in and applying it to someone else's company as an outside consultant.

"I had to learn to think as a CEO, rather than as a consultant. I had no clue what that took until I was thrown into the middle of our events and approaching them as the decision maker. That's why I placed such a strong emphasis on creating context with you earlier yesterday. Without it, you get sucked back into believing you're improving things — when you're actually reinforcing what you're trying to get rid of. That happened to me over and over again as a CEO.

"But, let's take your questions one at a time, Mitch, and see if I can cover in a few minutes what it took the plant three days to get to and three years to completely implement.

> "I HAD TO LEARN TO THINK AS A CEO . . . . I HAD
> NO CLUE WHAT THAT TOOK UNTIL I WAS THROWN INTO
> THE MIDDLE OF OUR EVENTS AND APPROACHING THEM
> AS THE DECISION MAKER."

A Shift in Causality

"FIRST IT REQUIRED A TOTAL SHIFT IN THEIR BELIEF ABOUT CAUSALITY. The major discovery for the plant manager was similar to your experience on the bridge. It was about where they placed their attention. Then they had to let go of what they were holding onto. Believe me, they had very hard-core beliefs about people, the plant, upper management, the Atlanta headquarters, other departments and each other. They even had beliefs about their ability to make any difference at all in the organization.

"They were always looking at what was going wrong; it was like you looking down at the bottom of the ravine. Fear consumed them and they reacted. Of course, none of them admitted being afraid. These were all hardened managers. They were tough guys."

Focus is the Essence of Structure

BILL WENT ON TO REMIND MITCH THAT THE ESSENCE of structure inside an organization is about focus. "Ultimately they discovered that if they developed and never violated a four-fifths philosophy of how they ran the plant, it would become and stay in balance. This took out the source of upset conditions that existed everywhere they looked. The four-fifths philosophy became their **Leverage Point**. It became the real Vision of the organization, just like Federal Express's Absolutely, Positively, Overnight — or 10:30 AM. Just like everyone at Fed Ex knows their job is to get it there by 10:30 AM every day, everyone at the plant became consumed with operating it at four-fifths capacity every day.

Leverage Points Result in a State of Balance

"Remember Mitch, a leverage point takes out upset conditions and results in a state of balance. Balance is the key to growing at an optimum rate. When a state of balance exists, you are aligned and maximizing resources...assets. Then you are totally productive. If something gets slightly out of balance, reactive behavior will eventually show up just about everywhere."

Bill recalled how, on his second visit to the plant, they discovered a buffer zone of eight hours out in the log yard that allowed this 24/7 operation to focus on what really mattered to them. It took a month of everyone focused on the four-fifth operating philosophy to be able to see the eight hour buffer zone leverage point. Then, maintaining absolute pressure on what was required to develop each person's competencies and bring them to a level where they could operate their area of responsibility with absolute excellence, became the final leverage point. Consequently, he related, they started focusing on inspired performance — without knowing what to call it at the time. He now defines **inspired performance** as *the idea generation coming from the front line that reduces cycle time and costs while increasing quality and service to customers (both internally and externally) in a high-spirited manner.*

"You must have had quite a willing organization to accomplish all of that when you first got there," Mitch said.

"Actually, that's a total other story, Mitch, but worth noting before we move on."

Then Bill related how, just two weeks before being asked to intervene at the plant, the plant manager's truck was turned upside down and burned in his parking space directly in front of the plant, and how — even after extensive police investigations — absolutely no one saw it happen. He recalled that three major unions existed inside the plant, all whom hated each other to such a degree that if the mechanical union went on strike the electrical union would come to work. If a family member from a union went into management, the rest of the family would not speak to them, although they often lived next door. He described it as a surreal world — much like the feuds between the Hatfields and McCoys must have been.

"You could say they were a bit hostile toward the ideas we're talking about today — especially any kind of philosophy or change in their way of thinking. Believe me, Mitch, that included the plant manager. He did not ask me to come. I was sent by corporate headquarters in Atlanta."

"YOU COULD SAY THEY WERE A BIT HOSTILE TOWARD THE IDEAS WE'RE TALKING ABOUT TODAY—ESPECIALLY ANY KIND OF PHILOSOPHY OR CHANGE IN THEIR WAY OF THINKING."

"That is really something, Bill. I thought we had some tough challenges. What did it take for all this change to take place?"

"The answer kept coming back to structure causes behavior. Actually, all we did was change the shape of the land. Many change initiatives were launched during the three years I worked with them. The management team literally became a design team. They began using the principles of structural thinking we're discussing now. They used them in every meeting.

"The biggest issue, however, was winning the trust of the entire work force. That challenge had to be accomplished one person at a time. One of our major change initiatives was the establishment of trust. We trained everyone — including the frontline people — how to build trust. Believe me when I say we had to deal with distrust issues. We had family conflicts, local politics, years of union conflicts, and mis-management. It seemed to never end. But after several months, all of a sudden it shifted, and people were aligned."

Bill related to Mitch how the unions opened up and began working together, and how they formed teams that focused on serving their customers. He revealed how, over time, they found that everyone wanted the same thing. They wanted to be a part of something bigger than themselves — something great. They wanted their ideas to be heard and implemented. They wanted to work together as a team. "The big discovery was that what they wanted was already inside of everyone. We just had to change the shape of the land so the water that was already there, inside of them, could flow."

"That's quite a story. What ultimately happened?"

"They started as a system that was controlled by the unions, which mainly focused on maximizing overtime and benefits for their members. Strong silos (with extremely high walls between every department) contained everything from politics, blame, and actual sabotage that often shut the place down. We were able to go from 40 supervisors to four with a 400 member workforce made up of the three unions. After a year, they became the most productive and highest quality performers in the division — and they had the oldest plant by at least 10 years. They did all of that without any of the technological modernizations that their newer sister plants were getting. They had originally been written off as a lost cause. But in the end, they demonstrated what they could accomplish by simply removing upset conditions and focusing on achieving a state of balance."

"That example sure gives me encouragement. Did SynergyCorp go through the same process?"

"Similar, Mitch. When I began working with them as one of our suppliers, I found they had done an incredible amount of work on making sure they had all the right people in the right jobs. I learned a lot from them. They were steadfastly focused on the development of people — they were already committed at the top level of the organization to being a great company.

"All I did was introduce the tools for structural thinking and the principles for achieving inspired performance. I suppose my being their biggest customer gave me some leverage, because they were all ears when I introduced to them the kind of supplier we needed them to be for us to grow our business. I let them know how important they were to us and they really responded. It was truly satisfying to create a supplier partnership with them.

"On the other hand, we approached other suppliers who seemed afraid we were just trying to extract lower price concessions from them. Those companies were reacting out of years of having been beaten down by their customers. At SynergyCorp, the owner was eager to form a true partnership. You need to meet him when you get back to Atlanta."

"Bottom line," Mitch said, "It is all about finding key leverage points that put things in balance, isn't it?

As Bill nodded in agreement, Mitch went on to relate that one of his courses as an undergraduate at MIT was geology, and that he could see an analogy between the constant pressure that exists in the earth causing a sudden shift to take place and the shift in trust between management and the workforce Bill experienced at the plant. He continued that, ironically, the shift we would call an earthquake or major event, isn't one at all. It is the result of a constant state of multiple pressures converging over time, until finally the movement in the earth shifts. "That's what I believe happened when the plant's management focused on creating trust between unions — one person at a time — until all of a sudden people were aligned.

"Although I believe in alignment, I have never realized the kind of pressure that it takes over time to achieve it. I've tried to achieve it by doing seminars, holding meetings and giving talks. Those things never really take hold, do they Bill? It takes actually changing the land. That's what happened in your plant. It took consistent pressure until the shift occurred. It came about because of their focus.

"THE SHIFT WE WOULD CALL AN EARTHQUAKE OR MAJOR EVENT ISN'T ONE AT ALL. IT IS THE RESULT OF A CONSTANT STATE OF MULTIPLE PRESSURES CONVERGING OVER TIME, UNTIL FINALLY THE MOVEMENT IN THE EARTH SHIFTS."

"So Bill," Mitch continued, "the first thing I need to do is get together with my team and chart our recurring patterns and identify where we have upset conditions. Then we'll use the patterns to reveal the underlying structure that causes them. Is that right?"

"That's right on. That simple process will take you from level one to level two, **seeing**. Part of the reason for charting the patterns and events is to see that what we react to, the problems we try to solve, are only a part of a recurring pattern. Do you remember the black dot from when we were talking about context? Events or problems are kind of like the black dot. They are just one moment of time in the entire pattern. It's probably easier to visualize if we make a drawing of it."

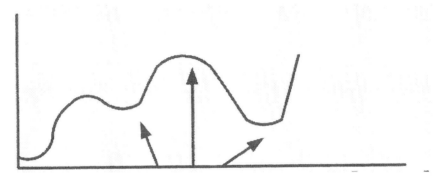

An <u>Event</u> is just part of a pattern, such as a drop or rise in sales, quality or production

Focus Determines Results

Back at the table, Bill continued. "When you take events out of context, they become a problem and cause a reactive state. Reactive states are like a snowball rolling down a hill. They have a life of their own. When you react to them, you actually reinforce and strengthen their hold on your thinking and behavior. They have their own underlying structure (which I will show you in a few moments), that causes more of the same. It goes back to the principle of focus: *whatever you focus on is what you produce*. Focus determines results. In this case, you get more of what you don't want. It often ends up in a lot of CYA behavior as people tend to find fault or place blame."

Mitch said reflectively, "That's what you mean by yesterday's solutions become today's problems."

"Exactly. Because you're focusing on what gets your attention, you'll

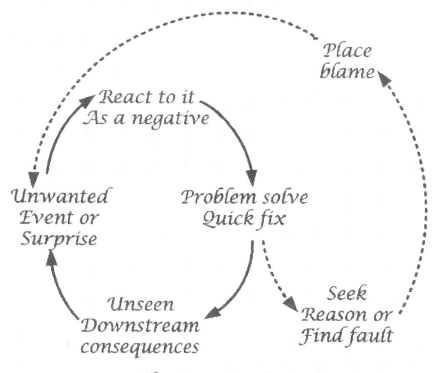

The Reactive Structure

not be able to give your attention to what will create the future.

"Here's an illustration of what I mean by the underlying structure that results from reacting to events."

"Can you see how this becomes a vicious circle and causes a snowball-rolling-down-a-hill effect? As it rolls downhill, it gains size and momentum. It can literally consume everything you do for days, even years. In some cases it causes an avalanche within the organization — like ending up in bankruptcy."

Bill expanded to say that the other thing about events, or what are called surprises or problems, is that they don't actually exist, but are a spec of time in a pattern that finally becomes so intense — or so much pressure builds up around it, like in Mitch's geological illustration — that they get attention and demand a quick response.

Still at the flipchart, he suggested, "Let's take a few critical areas to start and just focus on one aspect of the business for our purposes today. When we pull your entire team together we can do all of your critical areas and have everyone involved discover what we're discovering together. It is quite an experience to watch that happen. We'll chart every recurring pattern that exists inside your company."

Is that what you did with SynergyCorp?"

"Yes it is, but I didn't have the degree of understanding back then that I do now. Synergy's people are all quite unique in that they were selected based on their suitability for the job. They were both **eligible**, a concept we use to select employees, and they were **suitable**. That means not only *can they do the job*; we also know *they will do the job*… because they want to. They were open and excited to embrace our ideas. People there were chosen based on what they loved doing and what they were best at accomplishing. They had the right people on the bus. That's another vital discussion for us to have, but at a later time."

"Ok Bill, but I want to understand how they accomplished having the right people aboard. It generally takes us about 18 months to determine that we have selected or promoted the wrong person into a position. The cost of that has been horrendous. Can we take a little break first? I want to think about where we should start and what seems to be the most problematic."

During the break, Mitch strolled outside to take in the surrounding vista. He breathed deeply of the mountain air and soon felt rejuvenated. In spite of their intense discussions, he was eager to take an in-depth look at his own organization and was able to pinpoint key areas of concern.

When the two men were reassembled, Mitch began with a request. "Help me along here Bill, so that I can get going.

"I have several areas that are constantly getting our attention. We could easily begin with sales effectiveness, as revenue issues are regularly the topic of our management team strategy sessions. Customer service and productivity are close seconds. We also have personnel issues like turnover, interpersonal and departmental conflicts. Then there's quality, financial/cash flow, supplier issues and taking new products to market."

"Mitch, all of these areas will need to be charted and examined eventually."

"Well, they are all problems that we're 'solving' every day. They all become events that get our attention."

"... THIS BECOMES A VICIOUS CIRCLE AND CAUSES
A SNOWBALL-ROLLING-DOWN-A-HILL EFFECT ... IT GAINS
SIZE AND MOMENTUM. IT CAN LITERALLY CONSUME
EVERYTHING YOU DO..."

"You bet; nothing mysterious about them. But do you ever notice how, even though you have solved them, they keep coming back over and over again?"

"I do. And I remember telling my executive team the other day that solving problems is their job — it comes with being in this business. Problems are not going to go away. Even though we think we're solving new problems every day, it was discovered in one of our recent team building sessions that there were only a handful of problems that kept recurring. I guess we haven't solved them if they keep coming back, have we?"

"Good insight! By discovering that, you're ahead of the game. Let's start with sales effectiveness, because many things flow from there."

"I think you are right. If we could get our arms around this issue, it might resolve many of the others that we have as well."

"Think about it this way," Bill suggested, moving back to the flip-chart. "You've been growing rapidly — so what has increased? Then what has decreased as each of these areas has increased? Note all of those things that happen that are unwanted. I'll quiz you on the quick fix or reactive behavior and see if we can conclude what the long-term consequence of your reactive behavior might be."

Mitch thought about it for a moment. "Well, I would start with the number of accounts and the complexity of each order. Our success has resulted in an increase in the number of accounts each sales person has to manage. We were getting higher margins on custom work, so we really went after that. This has required more detailed specifications, of course. The amount of service time required on each account has increased dramatically. The complexity of each order and the number of changes from each client has also increased."

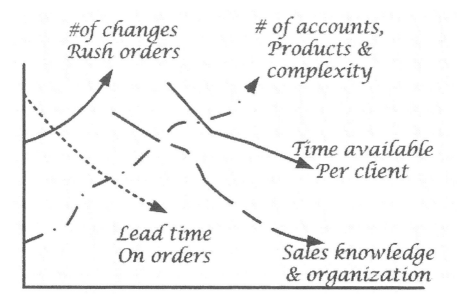

Sales success limits success of salesperson

For the next two hours, Mitch and Bill mapped out all of the patterns associated with Sales Effectiveness. Then they used those patterns to map out the underlying structure that caused them.

Note: This dialog is in the appendix if you want to see the level of detailed work they accomplished and the level of understanding that is possible when applying the tools for structural thinking.

CHAPTER 8 *Organizations Work Perfectly— Exactly the Way They Are Designed*

At the conclusion of their last session, Bill had moved to the great picture window where he reflected quietly for a few moments, then turned to address Mitch.

"The only way any organization can work is the way it is designed to. Based on that concept, all organizations work perfectly. They produce what they are designed to produce — even if it's what you don't want.

"What we've just charted are patterns of behavior that you don't want. They are all upset conditions that ultimately have limited your growth."

Distinguishing between Organizational Behavior and Structure

LETTING THAT SINK IN, BILL EXPLAINED, "THE PATTERNS WE have charted demonstrate **organizational behavior**. Behavior changes over time. It needs to be clearly distinguished from structure. **Structure** is how the organization is made. It causes behavior and is the blueprint for how an organization is designed. It determines how all of the parts relate to each other. So now we'll map out the structure by using the patterns we've charted as our guide.

Casual Feedback Loops

"THE FIRST THING WE'LL DO IS BUILD THE CORE, or foundational **causal feedback loop** of the organization. That is what we refer to as the **underlying structure**. Remember that I said we would use the three insights, a few principles and the laws of nature to evaluate it. This is where the laws of nature clearly come into view.

"As much as I look forward to understanding the source of all these patterns," Mitch said, "it is hard to grasp that the organization is working perfectly if it produces what I do not want."

After a pause, he continued, "Wait a minute. Something just hit me like a ton of bricks. When you just now mentioned the laws of nature, I realized I have been violating everything my father taught me. As you know, I grew

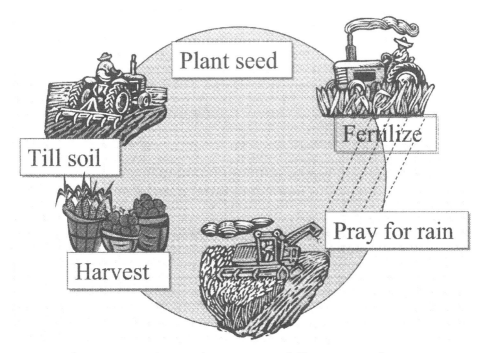

up on a farm. He taught me that to successfully grow anything, you must first prepare the soil in the fall and let it sit in the winter. Then you can plant your seeds in the spring and care for their growth by irrigating throughout the summer. Only then can you have an abundant harvest in the fall.

"This is what you are referring to as a law of nature, isn't it? I can see how it's the real underlying structure of growing a successful business. We have violated this simple truth over and over, and I believe that's caused many of the patterns we just charted. When it was time to harvest, we decided to hurry up and plant. Our entire sales effectiveness strategy, as you called it, was not a strategy at all. It was driven by my need to increase sales and go after the high-margin accounts. The very thing we were doing to grow our sales was causing the upset conditions we mapped out that limited our growth."

Walking over to join Bill at the window, Mitch continued, "I tried to teach this to my two kids about studying. Mark really got it, but John, my younger son, never did. When John had a test, he would study on the way to school that morning. It would get me so frustrated and angry every time it happened.

"You know Bill, I am exhausted and somewhat embarrassed by all of this. I can see that our situation was caused by violating a law that I know in my heart to be the source of life. Rather than growing the organization, I've been destroying it."

Organizational Learning Disabilities

"LISTEN, MITCH, DON'T BE SO HARD ON YOURSELF. IN THE SYSTEMS DYNAMICS world, the inability to see is called a **learning disability.** One such disability is called the boiled frog syndrome. You know how to boil a frog, don't you?"

Mitch laughed. "Sure. Actually, I used that example in a speech at the GT Leadership Academy. You place the frog in a pot of cool water and slowly increase the heat — which they don't seem to notice. Soon you have a boiled frog. I get that we are, in fact, boiled frogs. This all happened over time and we didn't see it taking place. We were focused on growth and beating the competition and doing what it took to prepare for our IPO (so we could really grow the business). I guess our growth strategy almost became our exit strategy. It could literally have been over for us earlier this week. If SynergyCorp hadn't stepped up with their support and parts, the banks could have shut us down."

"I know this has all been tough. Another concept is called **group think**, which I believe often happens when there is a charismatic leader, like yourself, at the helm. Sadly, in most organizations, the level of thinking that takes place is not exceptional. Trying to look good, fear of making mistakes, conflicts, defensiveness, and politics all get in the way of thinking clearly and learning from past experiences. The focus is on ones' own agenda. When this is happening, it's hard to stand back and see these patterns and causal structures. That's because cause and effect are separated by time and space. It's difficult to see how they are connected.

> "... CAUSE AND EFFECT ARE SEPARATED BY
> TIME AND SPACE."

The Emperor's New Clothes

"THE OTHER THING THAT OCCURS WHEN YOU HAVE A POWERFUL LEADER is 'the emperor's new clothes' syndrome. No one will tell the emperor that the new clothes he has on are not real. There is a very strong tendency to tell the boss what he wants to hear — that his ideas are wonderful. To speak up is seen as 'not being on the team.' I suspect you get a lot of that."

Moving back to the conference table, Bill suggested, "Since we don't have a lot more time to work together this weekend, I'd like to cover a few other critical things before you leave."

Seeing over Time, Space and Causality

"As we discussed earlier, most people view life from a reactive context instead of a generative one. When you change your context you can begin to see everything over time, as we are doing here. Once we map everything out, cause and effect are no longer separated by time and space. We can see the past, the present and the future all at one moment in time. That makes for a very powerful way of seeing and thinking. It completely changes all decision making."

Bill moved to the wall, which was now completely covered with the charts he and Mitch had worked on. He pointed out that now, by working with his underlying structure, Mitch would be able to see the consequences of every decision — even before he made it. He emphasized that once the rest of the strategies were mapped out and combined, he would have a flight simulator that would allow him to see the cause of the patterns he had charted and change things before they happened. It was clear that they had grown too large too fast. They grew beyond their capacity and capability in many areas.

"What is distressing to me, Bill, is that at the time we thought we were being strategic," Mitch offered with an air of frustration.

"That's okay," Bill said encouragingly. "Notice that each of your upset conditions is caused by (or at least amplified by) attempting to increase sales and revenue before developing capacity. Trying to grow too quickly often takes you beyond your capacity and ultimately results in slowing actions. The principle behind this is to *never grow beyond your capacity and capabilities*. Maintain your focus on development. There are no short cuts or methods that work in the long run. They violate the laws of nature."

The Cure is Often Worse Than the Disease

BY WAY OF ILLUSTRATING HIS POINT, Bill referred to some farmers who attempted to deal with insects that were eating away at their crops. As a quick fix, they sprayed on pesticides to protect their harvest. It worked in the short run and they continued the practice. Over time, the insects that naturally ate the bugs feeding on the plants were completely killed, while the plant-eating insects developed immunity to the pesticides and flourished. Stronger remedies were taken and even more spraying resulted. Finally, the entire water table below the once-fertile land was unfit for drinking or irrigation as it, too, became a carrier of the pesticides. "The cure was far worse than the cause," he concluded.

Nodding in agreement, Mitch recalled having read about some other farmers who nurtured the growth of insects who ate plant-eating insects. They reported losing some of their crops during the first year, but by the second year they achieved a balanced state. Not only did they have healthier crops, without pesticides, but they also had clean water. "It took two years for them to change the pattern that was in place and put things back into balance.

"Anyway, going back to my situation," Mitch continued, redirecting the conversation for his own clarity, "as orders reached a certain level, a backlog was created due to a lack of engineering and exhausted production capacity, as well as other capability issues. The backlog then began increasing over time, causing customer perception to drop further. The more we tried to 'do what ever it takes' to serve these upset customers, we created more problems in manufacturing and engineering. Basically the more we did to keep from losing a client, the more we were exacerbating our production capacity.

"Because I thought we had a sales problem, we offered more discounts to clients and incentives to our sales team to get sales back up. Yet the incentives seemed to make it worse. Talk about a vicious circle!"

"THE MORE WE TRIED TO 'DO WHAT EVER IT TAKES' TO SERVE THESE UPSET CUSTOMERS... THE MORE WE WERE EXACERBATING OUR PRODUCTION CAPACITY."

Picking up one of the markers, Mitch offered, "Let me see if I can map out what we have just discussed. I believe this is the underlying structure of what we just described."

Without waiting for Bill's response, he continued, "You know Bill, at the GT Leadership Academy, we played the MIT Beer Game and were able to

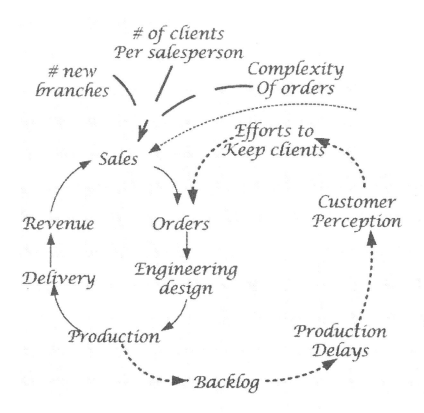

see the Beer Game effect or vicious circles throughout our operations. That is what I see right now everywhere I look. A bunch of vicious circles. I think it would be great to play the beer game with my team when we get back to Atlanta. That really gets these points across.

"Also, I did a quick estimate, and I believe that almost 85 percent of management time is spent in reactive behavior — or fire fighting — much like your plant that was out of control."

Pointing to one of the charts on the wall, Mitch elaborated further. "Right about here it seems, we were making sales that were beyond the experience, knowledge and skill level of our people, both in engineering and in sales. Even those on the front line were incapable of keeping up with or resolving our customer problems.

"So right here, sales finally began to flatten out; when we examined things more closely, they had actually dropped in some of the branches. Therefore, we increased our sales efforts and gave incentives to our clients, including discounts,

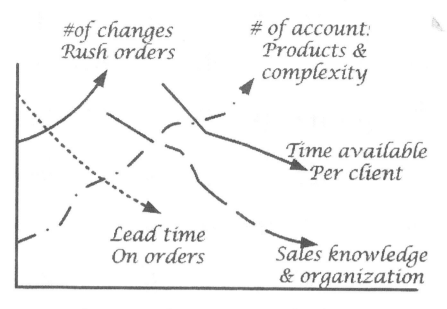

Sales success limits success of salesperson

in order to regain our sales momentum. It worked for a while and we thought we had solved the sales problem. In reality we made it worse. Like the farmers, we sprayed more and more pesticides on the crops and ruined the water table under the ground. Our cure was worse than the original symptoms."

"Excellent evaluation, Mitch. Now let's focus on the consequences resulting from those fix-it solutions."

Mitch took a deep breath, then offered, "Okay, let's see. We experienced lower quality and had to do more and more rework and redo. Then we spent a huge amount of time trying to satisfy customers we were about to lose. We actually gave credits and deductions, plus sent our most experienced engineers into the field to work directly with them."   *L & T*

"One little redo can upset things and throw the entire company out of balance, can't it?" Bill sympathized.

Nodding, Mitch continued, "Right here you can see where customer (and engineering) changes in orders doubled — in some cases tripled. It all happened when we started increasing order complexity by offering more and more customized work. The amount of time needed to process an order must have become five times what it had been on a single, simple project."

BIR

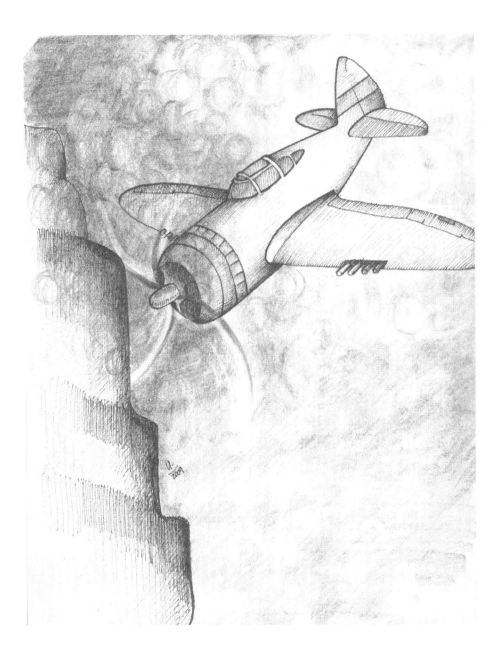

Mitch pointed to a particular spot on a chart. "The costs started escalating right about here. Then financial pressures started to take their toll as customers delayed their payments. Costs seemed to grow exponentially while at the same time our quality standards fell below expectations."

Organizational Vertigo

HE PAUSED FOR A MOMENT IN DEEP THOUGHT. "We thought we were heading into the clouds — we were still achieving our sales objectives quarter after quarter. Truth is, we were continually trying to dig our way out of a deeper and deeper hole."

"That's a typical case of **organizational vertigo**, Mitch, and you're not alone. Lots of CEOs are deceived by sales figures. They believe they are flying into blue skies, when they're actually crashing into the side of a mountain. Believe me, you are not the only CEO that's been intoxicated and blindsided by increasing sales numbers. Nevertheless, when you're in a hole, it's a good idea to stop digging." They both laughed, and it broke the tension of what was a difficult realization for Mitch.

"Now you can see the power of knowing your underlying structure. And all we have looked at here is your Sales Effectiveness Strategy. Do you see other things that were happening that made the situation worse?"

"Well, our sales people get sucked into all of these problems, giving them less face time with new customers. They spend most of their time trying to save existing accounts. I guess that represents the quick fix and problem solving you mapped out. After a great deal of overtime (and finger pointing between departments) we eventually got caught up. In the interim, we lost credibility with some of our major accounts, forcing us to scale back and delay our plans for new branches."

"Nice job, Mitch. You're really getting a grasp on these concepts."

"There's another area that just jumps off the page," Mitch said with a heavy sigh. "Our customer service is under all kinds of pressure as well. A high level of experience in customer service is essential. It is a real pressure cooker environment. Not many people are well suited for it, I guess, because we're experiencing high turnover. This causes its own set of difficulties between customers, engineering, production, scheduling and transportation."

Looking intently at one of the charts, Mitch admitted, "I can see that what we've mapped out happens repeatedly. These are patterns. They exist because of the reactive way we've been doing business."

"Now you're starting to get into the other Six Strategies we discussed earlier, that make up the complete organizational structure."

"Unfortunately, we've only looked at one small area of our systems so far."

"Mitch, let's talk separately about systems. It's easy to confuse systems with the underlying structure of the organization. There is a significant difference in that the underlying structure is made up of multiple systems and business processes."

The Perfect Storm

"I CAN'T WAIT TO MAP OUT WHAT HAPPENS WHEN WE'RE BRINGING new products to market and merging new acquisitions into the company," Mitch said with a good deal of sarcasm.

"I think it will make the sales effectiveness issues look like a walk in the park. These are the issues that make it difficult for me to sleep at night and cause me anxiety when I wake up. Now add our financial crisis to that — along with our suppliers going through a worse time than the previous year — and you have a real disaster on your hands. It is the perfect storm."

Structure Causes Behavior

"YES IT IS," BILL RESPONDED WITH CONCERN. "Now, imagine for a moment that suppliers have their own underlying structure and are also reacting to events — many of which come from you, their customer. Can you see how the underlying structure we've mapped out has caused the patterns we charted?"

They both stood for several minutes just reexamining the patterns they had charted.

"I see it," Mitch replied, shaking his head affirmatively. "Unfortunately, it totally describes our company. On the upside, now that I can see these time histories are caused by an underlying structure, I can predict how something is going to behave in the future — before reacting to any situation. Using this kind of data, I can almost see how your navigational guidance system could tell you where you were heading, before you even launch a new initiative."

To Change Behavior, Change the Underlying Structure

STUDYING THE TIME HISTORIES AND MAPS OF THE STRUCTURE THAT CAUSED THEM, Mitch continued, "It seems to me that these patterns are not going to change unless we can change the underlying structure. I mean — I've done everything possible to improve our processes in these areas and nothing really helped. In some cases, what we did to improve things — and they definitely were not quick fixes — has made matters even worse." Sheepishly he added, "Just a few days ago I remember thinking that our suppliers going out of business had nothing to do with us. I believed it was not our fault. But the truth is we caused many of the events they reacted to, just to keep our business. And now they're history. Boy, talk about a vicious circle coming around to bite us in the rear. Our solution has truly become our latest problem. I blamed 9 /11, my suppliers, the Dutch takeover competitors, my bankers and venture capital team — when all the while — I was the cause!"

"Unfortunately, without seeing these causal relationships by mapping them out this way, it's virtually impossible to have any degree of control or to know where to place your attention," Bill said sympathetically.

> "WITHOUT SEEING THESE CAUSAL RELATIONSHIPS BY MAPPING THEM OUT, IT'S VIRTUALLY IMPOSSIBLE TO HAVE ANY DEGREE OF CONTROL OR TO KNOW WHERE TO PLACE YOUR ATTENTION."

"What can we do about it? If you could solve this problem Bill, we would be able to dominate our industry. Everyone has the same issues. I sit with the executive committee of the industry leaders and we calculated that close to 80 percent of our production, engineering and sales capacity is absorbed by these same problems. It doesn't matter which company we're dealing with, large or small. Even some of our mom and pop competitors complain they're faced with the same kinds of issues. The difference is quantitative, not qualitative. Most of them think we're the best of the lot. That's scary, isn't it?"

"Mitch, do you notice how you've started addressing these conditions as problems and events again? When I was still running our division, you'd ask for my forecasts and budgets and I would tell you I was trying to figure out the underlying structure and cause of issues so I could accurately forecast and be predictive. I was working to map out the causal feedback loops to determine the source of the upset conditions and what was limiting our growth. Right now, it's essential that I jerk you back into the original context we set before we looked at the patterns and mapped out the underlying structure."

Mitch rose from the table with a heavy sigh. After a moment or two of contemplation at the picture window, he turned to face Bill. "Thanks for the feedback. You're right. I'm right back into reacting to them. I'm even thinking about how to get you to come solve them for me," Mitch admitted with an embarrassed laugh. "That's why I was so willing to go through literal hell to put in our new SAP software systems and implement a total quality program. The Six Sigma program required us to train every employee for over 40 to 50 hours last year. We spared no cost, thinking we were addressing the quality issues and getting ready to sell globally. They all promised to solve the problem (and I believe they thought they were). Instead we applied a bandage. We were just addressing a symptom — we were not addressing the actual cause."

Beware of Better Before Worse and Expect Worse Before Better

As he started to pace, Mitch emphasized, "Bill, I hope you hear me when I say I will do whatever it takes to change this. But I have to tell you — right now, it's really difficult to imagine that these problems don't exist. They are very real to me. They have not gone away as we have talked. They seem relentless right now."

Pausing for a moment, Mitch continued. "On one level, I feel somewhat enlightened, but on the other, I feel sick to my stomach. As we mapped this out (and even as we speak) I'm thrown right back — knee-deep — into them. Even after all we've talked about and what I have been through these past two days, I am emotionally caught up in it. It's actually quite depressing to see things in this manner."

Then he took a deep breath. "I will grant you this though. It's a little easier for me to see that the solutions we implemented may have actually reinforced and strengthened our 'problems.' I can also see the vicious circle and snowball effect you were talking about in several places in our underlying structure.

"However," he countered, "some of these things seem to be totally out of our control. They have a life of their own. I remember thinking earlier this week, even before I called you, that there was something else running our company. I didn't have a clue what it was, but I did know that I couldn't harness it and no matter what we did with outside consultants, we were not able to get its cause."

116

Thoughtfully, Mitch looked over the charts and graphs before him, stopping before one of them. "This is the one. It's like a vicious circle that determines everything we do.

"But what can be done? Has anyone else been able to reverse these patterns? How do you change an underlying structure?" Mitch challenged, agitated and pacing again.

Then he abruptly stopped, and his entire countenance softened. "Wait a second. Isn't that one of the three insights? When you change the underlying structure, the energy will flow according to the path of least resistance. Based on that, we can create what we want by simply changing the underlying structure."

Almost instantly, doubt crept back in. "This stuff really sounds abstract in light of the real problems we're faced with," Mitch confessed, "and we haven't even dug into the other issues that I consider my major challenges. I mean I have some real dilemmas to resolve yet."

"Mitch, almost everything you did made things better for a while, but as you discovered after we mapped everything out, they actually made things worse. To make the changes you want will usually result in a condition called 'worse before better.' It will take time to get things back in balance and become the way we want them to be. It will require steadfast focus while working with the laws of nature and the principles of structural design."

CHAPTER 9 *Aligning Around Leverage Points*

Focused on the vast vista before him, Mitch stood in quiet reflection before speaking again. "You know, Bill, I don't think most CEO's have a clue about the source of the difficulties they face. I know I sure didn't. I thought I had a cash flow problem when I came up here. I was faced with the difficulties of competition and suppliers and the economy. Man, I wasn't even close to addressing what was really going on and causing our difficulties. These things are long term, deeply rooted, and very, very subtle. They're definitely not where we tend to look."

"I WASN'T EVEN CLOSE TO ADDRESSING WHAT WAS
REALLY GOING ON. . ."

Cause is Invisible

"IT'S EYE-OPENING TO REALIZE THAT CAUSE BY ITS VERY NATURE, can't be seen. It's invisible. It's all rooted in these principles and laws we've been exploring, isn't it? That takes us right back to the organizational blindness, addictions and arrogance we discussed when we first started on this journey. When you add learning disabilities, like the boiled frog syndrome and the vertigo I had, I can see how it's next to impossible to think this way or see what we've mapped. It takes a completely different set of tools.

"You're right on, Mitch. That's what they're called — tools for structural thinking. And here's one of the greatest paradoxes of all: when someone is reacting to an event that has gotten their attention, it is 'next to impossible' for them to come remotely close to addressing the cause without using these tools.

"Tell you what Mitch, let's not dig into the other issues you have today. If we can discover the leverage points for this set of loops, the downstream effect will address many of the other concerns you have. After all, we want to build this same level of awareness, discovery and development for your management team and the rest of your individual contributors — especially if we're going to achieve inspired performance. They, too, must see it and feel the consequences of it, before the shift can take place that is required to bring about lasting organizational change."

100 Fires Don't Require 100 Solutions

As he stood to join Mitch at the picture window, Bill reiterated that one of the principles executives and managers often violate is in their belief that if there are one hundred fires, there must be one hundred solutions. Fortunately, that's not the case. He explained further that focus and alignment around one or two simple leverage points will address all one hundred fires. "In other words, it'd be far better to remove the source of the oxygen for all the fires, and therefore focus your attention on just one leverage point, than rush around, gobbling up precious resources attempting to put out all the fires.

The Cure Can Be Worse Than the Cause

"I think it's also vital to be aware that most any quick-fix solution has an amplifying effect anywhere it's applied. It often creates multiple new problems everywhere; it's not a one-to-one ratio. A simple reaction to an insignificant 'event' can have a highly counter-productive, even destructive impact on the entire organization. This is clearly a paradoxical relationship, where the cure is worse than the cause."

Moving back to the flipchart, Bill continued, "Let's see if we can stand back and discover a few leverage points that will remove the upset conditions you are experiencing before you leave here."

Somewhat skeptical, Mitch asked, "How do you go about discovering them, Bill? I'm really at a loss as to where to begin. Once again, I'm not even sure I know what you're talking about yet when you refer to leverage points. I'm constantly using leverage to get things done, but I don't think that's what you're referring to."

"Remember the plywood plant—they were constantly in a reactive mode. Yet once they went through this process they discovered that if they adopted a four-fifths philosophy everywhere in the plant and created an eight hour buffer zone in the log yard they could remove the source of almost all patterns of upset conditions."

"What does a four-fifths philosophy or a buffer zone have to do with a leverage point for my business? Even though I seemed to understand what you said when you told the story, I still don't have a clue about what a leverage point is."

Playing "What if"

"LET'S PLAY 'WHAT IF' FOR A FEW MINUTES. There are only a couple of places to look for leverage points, but to be able to find them you need to understand how your feedback loops actually work and how the principles behind them operate. Let's use your story about the law of nature. Imagine that a farmer wanted to harvest in the fall but he neglected to plant his seeds until the end of the summer or the early fall, just before harvest. What would happen?"

"Well, if you planted late," Mitch answered, willing to play along, "the seed would not have time to germinate or assimilate. It wouldn't have a chance to absorb nutrition from the soil, sun, rain or fertilizer. Is that what you looking for?"

"Precisely, Mitch. Anything that violates the laws of nature will fail to produce the intended results or certainly prevent you from attaining an optimum growth rate. It would not result in the desired abundant harvest. The same is true with organizations, departments, people, and relationships. In our case, of course, the production capacity of each person also has a very high impact on all of this."

"You mean training and development."

"Yes, that's a big part of developing production capacity. It's like your father's laws of nature.

Identifying Leverage Points

"SO, WHEN LOOKING FOR LEVERAGE POINTS, what we're looking for is any area where some fundamental principle is being violated. For example, (1) growing beyond your capacity (2) not focusing on developing the necessary core competencies (3) exceeding production capacity, etc. Ask yourself, what is the source of your delivery delays? What effect do they have on customer perception? Any or all of these will ultimately have a long-term devastating impact on sales effectiveness when they are present. Sometimes you can have a perfect storm and all of them are in full force, driving the organization into financial bankruptcy or at the very least, heavy deficit spending to stay alive."

"Well, I believe I have a perfect storm going on inside my company. As I look at my underlying structure, I can see where we have excessive delivery delays, because we have focused on growing too fast…"

The Optimum Rate of Growth and Competency Development

"No Mitch," Bill interrupted, "not growing too fast, just beyond your production capacity. It's important how we talk about things at this point."

"Thanks, Bill. I think that's the second or third time you've had to put me back in my place."

"But you're right—the focus needed to be on developing competencies. Competency development ultimately will determine any organization's optimum rate of growth. It's your equation. It would be very rare if you were to find the leverage point for your sales effectiveness issues inside of your sales department. Don't try to solve sales inside a 'broken' sales department. Look elsewhere.

"A leverage point will almost always work like a thermostat works to regulate the temperature inside your home or office.

"Say you want the ideal temperature to be 68 degrees. The thermostat will click on the heat for a while when it is at 66, then after the heat is at 70, it clicks off. Once the air has cooled to 66 it clicks back on. Here is what that looks like."

"Inside the Plywood Plant, their leverage point was operating at four-fifths capacity. That was

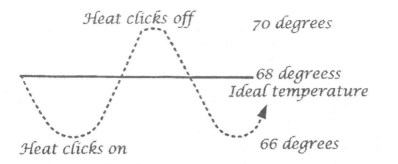

their temperature setting. The eight hour buffer zone in the log yard operated the same identical way."

"Let me try again—armed with your description of a leverage point as a thermostat. When we bought a second and third company, we were not able to assimilate them effectively. Each one of them has taken precious resources away from our core business. We've not developed the production capacity to meet our demand—and to top it off—we've been making sales promises to get more new business. All of this has placed incredible pressure on sales, production and engineering. Fundamentally, we're operating way beyond our capability. We also made price concessions to get the large customers who have more complex demands. When we won those accounts, we actually lost the margins necessary to increase our production capability.

"When I think about it," Mitch continued, shaking his head sadly, "We had healthy margins from our smaller accounts, yet more or less abandoned them when we landed the large ones. Everything we did that we considered to be our great successes carried with them significant downsides.

The Consequences of Being Out of Balance

"We definitely are not growing the business at an optimum rate. We seem out of balance. Best I can tell, the kind of pressure that drove much of that came directly from me. I made commitments to our investors. I had to make our numbers and show them that we were growing at the rate I told them we would, in order for them to continue to invest in our strategy. It seems that we violated the laws of nature at every turn."

"Determining the source of your out-of-balance state is where you may

..d your leverage points, Mitch. To say the least, you certainly are planting in the late fall, hoping to harvest immediately—maybe before you have even planted—in many cases. That's definitely in your nature. There's nothing you think you can't accomplish, just because you say it can be done." They both laughed.

"You're clearly getting how this works. It took me several years to gain the insights you have already demonstrated today. In other words, sometimes growing slowly in order to develop, assimilate and absorb nutrients results in the greatest harvest and often ends up being the optimum rate of growth…."

"And growing fast or beyond your production capacity is what shuts you down completely," Mitch interrupted, completing Bill's statement. "I can see that at best it ends up being counterproductive and self-limiting, causing upset conditions. It certainly was for us."

"Now you're zeroing in on the key issue: to seek the source of your upset conditions and remove it through a developmental process. You'll find that focusing on leverage points always requires placing and maintaining your attention on that one 'source' area, consistently over time, until it's back in balance. You want to pinpoint anything that throws the organization into an out-of-balance state."

Out-of-Balance Causes Domino Effect

"WHEN ANYTHING IS OUT OF BALANCE, JUST LIKE WHEN A CAR'S WHEELS are out of alignment, everything starts to shake. This causes a domino or snowball effect throughout the organization.

"There's a rate of growth in every organization where the wheels literally

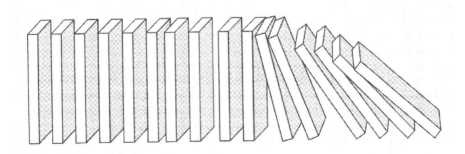

start coming off due to not addressing these mission-critical le
Anything that you can trace back to the cause of reactive behav
be considered a leverage point.

"There's an old saying, 'Anytime a butterfly flaps it wings in Japan, it causes a tornado in Oklahoma.' So any slight reaction or out-of-balance condition can have an overwhelming impact on an entire organization without you even knowing it. It is separated in both time and space so it's very difficult to make the connection between cause and effect.

"Even things that you avoid or just put off till later, due to other more critical problems or events that are getting your attention, can have a dramatic domino effect.

Organizations are Vulnerable to Wrong Thinking

"MITCH, YOU KIND OF HAVE TO LOOK AT IT THIS WAY: individuals are almost indestructible, with a very powerful immune system to fight off most any virus or condition. An organization, however, is so sensitive and vulnerable that even the wrong way of thinking about things by an executive can doom it to extinction. An organization can be killed off due to most any action that throws it into an out-of-balance state. Any growth that takes it beyond its capacity to serve its clients with the highest level of service can have the same effect. Depending on a company's size, the loss of one vital employee, client or supplier can have the same catastrophic effect. Very few new companies survive for very long….and if they continue in business…they're usually achieving a minimal amount of what they're capable of actually harvesting."

The Reason for Failure

"But don't most companies fail due to a financial crisis? It's the lack of cash to fund changes, new product development or whatever allows them to compete with the big players. I know in the CEO group that I participate in that's all I hear from them. They're either forced to sell their business or downsize it so severely that it loses its' vitality and ability to grow. In fact, that's all they're hearing from me right now, and we're the biggest player in our industry."

Then as an afterthought Mitch added, "In a sense, being the biggest player has made us the most vulnerable, even though we're feared by our competitors."

Bill agreed that businesses can't keep their doors open without the cash needed to keep going. "But that's like saying everyone dies because their hearts finally give out." he added. He went on to explain how most evidence reveals that heavy funding and cash reserves can hide an incredible amount of reactive and unconscious decision making that tends to amplify their difficulties. Having cash on hand can, in itself, be a source of bad decision making.

"They often can't see it until it's too late. I know CEO'S that are literally putting a gun to their company's feet (maybe even its head) and pulling the trigger, while thinking they're growing their business or making an intelligent decision. If it just affected the CEO that would be one thing, but it pulls their employees, suppliers and sometimes their customers down with them. Mitch, that's why I must do what I'm doing with my life right now. I think what I have learned is vital, and I must share it."

"You are a man on a mission," he responded with a warm smile.

The Tools for Structural Thinking

"ALTHOUGH WE'RE NOT WORKING IN YOUR COMPANY RIGHT NOW, WE'RE WORKING on it," Bill continued emphatically. "More importantly, we're working on it at a causal level from which we can actually change the future. From this vantage point, we have the high ground—like the warrior chiefs sought when going into battle.

"The discussion and analysis that we're doing right now is critical for you personally, Mitch. As you begin utilizing these tools for structural thinking you become your organization's highest personal leverage point. This is directly due to your way of thinking about things. The way you think must be based on a set of principles and laws."

The Highest Leverage Belongs to the Designer

FLIPPING BACK TO THE FIRST CHART WITH THE FIVE STEPS to overcoming organizational blindness, Bill stated, "When we're addressing leverage points that will change the future, we're at the fourth level of generative vision. Right now,

5. See yourself as the designer of the organization

4. See leverage points; align the organization around them

3. See underlying structure (causality) made up of control feedback loops

2. See patterns and trends that are increasing and decreasing over time—recognize there are no problems or events

1. See what others see that causes a reactive state to exist: recurring events, problems, quick fixes, long term consequences

you're at the fifth level, functioning like an architect or the designer of a ship."

"As you know, Mitch, I'm a sailor. We talked on my boat before I decided to sell my company to you. Do you remember?"

"Of course, how could I forget?"

"Do you remember the America's Cup race where the USA lost to Australia?"

"I do. Wasn't it off the East Coast back then?"

"Yes, Newport, Rhode Island… and that race changed sailing forever. Australia II was winning all the races when there were light winds and the Liberty, the USA defender, was winning during the heavier winds. Nobody could figure out what was going on. When it was discovered what happened, it was too late for the US to recover, and we've not yet caught up. Australia II had a winged keel design that provided sufficient hydrodynamic lift without the conventional large keel, which gave the advantage during the light winds to Australia. During the seventh and deciding race the winds turned light and the Australia II sailed to victory. It was won in the design tunnel, not on the sea.

Achieving Competitive Advantage

"THE AUSTRALIA II TEAM HAD CHARTED THE WIND PATTERN off the coast of Newport during that time period and found that 65 percent of the time there were light prevailing winds. They designed their keel specifically for light winds. That was their competitive edge, given everything else being equal.

Above the water, everything looked the same. The boats were identical; below the water line there were very subtle differences that created the competitive advantage.

"The Australians weren't just great sailors *working in the boat*; they were great designers, *working on it*. Now, that's where races are won and lost—in advance preparation, design and strategy. What won the race was the design of the underlying structure of the sailboat. They also had to build an organization that was totally aligned around developing a superior keel for the conditions of the water and the wind. They spent more time in the wind tunnel, in the design process with architects, than they did on the ocean. It's all about where they placed the focus of their attention."

The Highest Leverage Belongs to the Designer

"Great analogy." As Bill continued, he moved quickly to the flip chart pages taped on the wall. "Now, let's imagine that we just placed the right amount of attention in the right place for the right amount of time, in order to change the direction of the patterns we charted in your company. Using your example of the pressures in the earth that eventually cause a shift in the land we call an earthquake — let's exam-

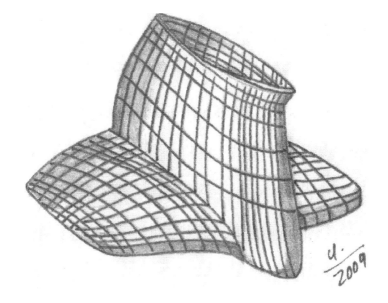

"THEY DESIGNED THEIR KEEL SPECIFICALLY
FOR LIGHT WINDS. THAT WAS THEIR COMPETITIVE EDGE . . .
ABOVE THE WATER, EVERYTHING LOOKED THE SAME."

ine your organization's underlying structure and see if we can determine where you should place your attention to reverse many of the patterns of reactive behavior. As you examine the organization's underlying structure, where would that be? What impact would that have on the patterns that we charted?"

"Based on what we've already discussed, it's definitely on developing our competency to deliver more complex and customized products to our clients. That single leverage point is what dictates our optimum rate of growth. The focus must shift to internal development, not external sales efforts. I can see how my desire to be the biggest and grow market share led to a completely wrong focus. All of our compensation systems are geared to this same end. We didn't miss a trick. We brought in people to train our sales force how to close orders, when in reality we weren't ready for them. The sales training backfired on us. Due to wrong thinking we violated the trust of our clients in all respects, didn't we?"

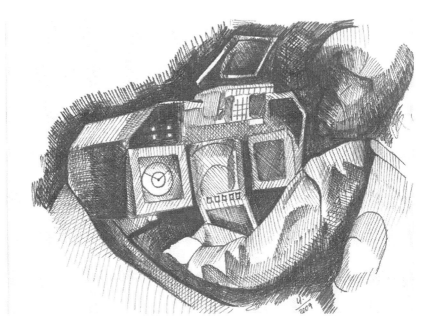

"NOW YOU CAN USE THE PRINCIPLES OF FLIGHT
TO DEVELOP YOUR ORGANIZATION."

"Listen, Mitch. Don't be so hard on yourself. You did great in identifying your leverage point. Now you can begin to think like an aeronautical engineer when designing a new plane. With all the feedback loops and time histories we've mapped out, you have a flight simulator of your organization. Now you can use the principles of flight to develop your organization. You literally have a flight simulator that allows you to grow your business at an optimum rate. You just have to learn to get into the cockpit and play 'what if' until you have the right strategy and have identified the managerial discipline necessary to execute it."

Rising from his chair, Bill concluded, "We've covered a lot so far today. Why don't you take a walk for a while and let all this sink in. If you're hungry there's fruit and cheese on the sideboard. Ask yourself, 'what kind of capabilities, competencies and discipline will it take to achieve the desired result'? You also need to think about the laws and principles that are operating here, and which ones need to be mastered and followed. Everyone back home will need to be aligned around them. Think about them, OK?"

Pausing before leaving the room, Bill added, "When we get back together, I'll be interested in your feedback and thoughts, especially your take on what we've covered and what you've discovered from all of this."

CHAPTER 10 *The Viewing Place*

Mitch walked out the door, his head buzzing with questions. Could all of the difficulties he had had be caused by the lack of focusing his attention on very simple leverage points? Were his company's difficulties really the result of unknowingly violating a few principles or failing to make some fundamental choices?

He headed off to his right and passed the sweat lodge. For some reason he stopped and sat on a rock and just looked at it, recalling his experience from the previous evening. "What caused time to stand still while I was in there?" he pondered. "I was in the lodge for several hours. I wonder if the cowboy was in there with me. It seems like it all happened so long ago, yet here I am being flooded emotionally, just as I was last night."

Immediately Mitch started to re-experience his time in the sweat lodge. Only this time it was different. His perspective had somehow shifted and he could now see patterns running throughout his life. Clearly he had his own personal out-of-balance conditions much like his organization did. He knew he had very rigid ways of thinking, making decisions, implementing projects and communicating. He had gotten feedback on all this, based on the 360 degree feedback sessions and evaluations he had received in the past. This was both, he was told, why he had been as successful as one of GT's young Turks, as he and a few others were called, but also why he had difficulties in his relationships. Now, he was afraid, it was why he was facing the dilemmas he had as a CEO.

Running things at GT was quite different from the challenges he was facing now. There, having a title really seemed to carry a lot of weight. It was like having the captain bars on his shoulder as an officer in Vietnam. Everyone followed orders. When you entered the room they stood. When you gave orders they said, "Yes Sir," and saluted. Now, as CEO, he felt he had no control, just a heavy burden to create shareholder value and get through one crisis after another. Again, he was overwhelmed with thoughts of survival. It was all he seemed to care about during this economic downturn.

"What's keeping me from seeing what I need to see?" he wondered. "What are my personal blind spots? What is my black dot?"

What is Most Simple is Most Profound

HE DECIDED THAT HE'D BETTER KEEP MOVING, as he didn't want to go through the emotional experience again that he had in the sweat lodge last night. As he walked, his mind no longer seemed to be thinking about problems or solutions anymore. All he could think about were the principles that he had somehow, unknowingly, violated that caused his organization to be out of balance. It was clear to him, as he thought about it, that something that simple could be totally defining. Then he remembered a statement that stuck with him from years ago: *What is the most simple is the most profound.*

Perhaps the key was as the cowboy had said when he was crossing the chasm, 'Just focus, Mr. Crandall. Let go — and move forward.'

"But within the organization," he pondered, "What do I focus on? I certainly don't see a knothole. Maybe my whole world has become a knothole. That was certainly what caused us to pursue top-line growth at any expense."

As he continued to walk, Mitch wrestled with jumbled thoughts and multiple questions. Bill asked him to think about lessons, principles and laws that they had discussed or he had experienced. He came upon a table in a clearing and sat down. After opening his planner where he had been taking copious notes he began underlining and numbering his thoughts.

"Well, the power of focus would be one. Whatever I focus on determines the results I end up with. Another would be that structure causes behavior. I see how these two principles actually build on one another. It seems to me that what I think about and focus on is also what determines the actual structure of the organization. Maybe my focus becomes the organization's underlying structure. Could that be what Bill is trying to get across? Bill's bottom line was that 'problems don't exist, but there are patterns caused by structure.' That's how we'll change those unwanted patterns we charted — by changing the structure. Is that how I change my focus?"

Mitch looked up at the deep blue sky and was taken back by the beauty of a huge bald eagle soaring above. He watched it for a few minutes in a sort of meditative state, wondering how many eagles he had killed off inside the organization. They seemed extinct. A couple of them had left to start their own companies and compete in the smaller markets.

his attention back to his notes, Mitch concluded, "First I need
[ ] my organizational blindness and see the pattern — like those
loops we drew — and identify the principles that were violated, causing the
out-of-balance conditions. I'm starting to see how everything is connected
— even how my way of thinking influences everything that goes on inside
the organization."

Initially, Mitch highlighted some of his notes, then he began organizing
them into chunks of useful knowledge. "If I'm going to really master these
principles, I'd better rewrite them and organize them so I can use them
when I return."

(See Appendix for Mitch's notes.)

for long term staff reduction

All We Can Control is Where We Place Our Attention

"Strange how, as I write these notes, I feel like I have no control over what
happens, yet I've put in control systems throughout my organization. Maybe
the only thing I actually can control is where I place my attention — that
seems to be what will determine the destiny of the organization."

Then his attention shifted. He began thinking about his suppliers. He
had required them to take at least 10 percent out of their cost to him each
year for the past five years, if they were to qualify as a premier supplier.
By doing that (while also requiring them to conform to his JIT standards)
he had hurt them financially. It had caused them to invest heavily to keep
his business. Then he bid out supplier contracts 'to keep them honest' and
'make them strong' by holding them accountable.

Heavy with remorse, Mitch could see how they were pawns in his
strategic game of growing his business on the backs of his suppliers. Now
several of them were gone.

"I don't think I've ever really thanked them for all they've done. I must
have created a great deal of fear in their lives. Did I do that to my own people? Did I do that to my boy, John? To Mark? Even to Charlotte? I guess the
fear inside of me was projected onto them, just like Bill said when talking
about my self-image....my circle of fear. None of that seemed conscious at
the time; I guess that's what is meant by the subconscious really determining what we do."

Would I like to hire short term JAVA (margin note)

The unsettling truth of his self-disclosure sent a sudden hot flash through his body. He started to walk again and continued to sort through things. "Inside the company, I know we're not aligned. We're not following these principles. We are far from being inspired. What else does it take to achieve inspiration? This is so different from simple management skills or any of the leadership training I used to conduct at the Institute."

Laws, Principles and Cause

"WHAT IS IT ABOUT ME THAT LIMITS OUR GROWTH? HOW HAS MY DECISION-MAKING and focus on events and problems — my rigid ways of doing things — caused upset conditions in the company? I came up here to learn about the company; somehow I keep asking questions about myself. I appear to be the source of it all."

It seemed to Mitch that when he focused on principles he was tapping into an inspired place he never knew existed. Now, as he thought about the people in his life, he could see an opportunity to serve their dreams. "I know that's why people originally joined our company. I really sold our vision to them and they had a dream. Now, I'm afraid they have substituted their dream for a paycheck. Not that I haven't held them accountable to achieve objectives. But whose goals are they, really? I'm afraid they're actually all mine. I wonder what theirs would be, if they had the freedom to pursue them."

IT SEEMED TO MITCH THAT WHEN HE FOCUSED ON
PRINCIPLES HE WAS TAPPING INTO AN INSPIRED PLACE
HE NEVER KNEW EXISTED.

Then it hit him. "Yes, I am somehow responsible. I am the cause of it all. No one else is to blame. Yet, up till now, I have even made my investors wrong for not stepping up with more money during this last crisis."

Mitch continued walking and felt something he could not recognize. "Excitement? No. Energy? Yes, I think so, but it's more than that. I feel completely connected to everyone in the organization right now. I want to sit down with all of them. One by one. They are what it's really all about —

their ideas. Just like with SynergyCorp helping us. They had a sense of ownership. Just like the cowboy working on the rope bridge to make it safer for the next person crossing that 1,000-foot deep ravine.

People Want to Contribute and Be Valued

"TO BE INSPIRED, PEOPLE NEED TO FEEL LIKE THEY'RE PART OF SOMETHING bigger than themselves. That's how I feel right now. I know people want to have a place to contribute. They want their ideas to really make a difference. That's how they connect. I can see them clearly now — wanting to make a contribution. They're all just like the SynergyCorp team who showed up with the parts on Thursday morning and stayed with it till they were shipped late Friday evening. Their energy was sky high after we got the orders out, even higher than our people's. I could tell that they loved being there to help us.

"And that one man, Joseph, thanked me for the opportunity to show up and actually see us implement his ideas. He saved us time, cut down on future warrantee claims, and even helped us assemble and ship our products. He embodies everything I want for our people. Their whole team of people did. No wonder Bill refers to them as 'contributors.'"

The contrast of those last two days was suddenly overwhelming. "What if we had just gotten our old parts shipped because the bank caved in to my latest threat? I can't believe I told them we wouldn't be able to pay them if they didn't give us a letter of credit to get our parts. Their new credit policy could have taken us under. Even though it seemed very true at the time, they were not responsible for our crisis and my dilemma. I was blaming them and making them responsible for our self-created crisis. Actually, it seems I was blaming everyone: the suppliers, consultants, bankers, our VC group, even my own executive team.

"What a nightmare that was. I actually got my banker, Don, out of his own birthday party. I was supposed to be there. When I called I sort of implied that our friendship was on the line over this one, and later that day he got me the letter of credit. Thanks to SynergyCorp I didn't need it. Boy, do I have some fences to mend when I get back to Atlanta."

As Mitch paused to gaze out at the purple mountains, he was enthralled with the vista that lay before him. He took in several deep

breaths of fresh mountain air and a feeling of exaltation rushed over him. Everything in his view seemed symbolic of what lay before him back home. "The freedom I feel right now, just saying those things, has caused me to feel light again. Just like I felt when I focused and crossed the chasm.

.en I left the sweat lodge. There's so much that I can see now. t this special place is having on me? But is it really that special? inside of me that all of this is happening? Is this why the Indian chieftains would come here to align their spirits? Who else has walked this path before me? Who is walking it with me now? Is everyone really inside of me and not out there?"

Mitch wandered for quite some time, and all he could see and think about were those he had failed to serve. He realized that he didn't even know what it was that they wanted. He had no idea of their dreams or goals. Yet that is what he now wanted to dedicate himself to seeing them achieve. "There must be a better way to manage people. Perhaps that's something else I need to master. Yet I'm not sure people really want someone managing them. They want someone in their life to help fulfill their dream."

Once again Mitch found himself at the rope bridge. This time he was all alone. By now the sun was setting, and the glare made it difficult to see the other side. For some reason, he felt compelled to step up on the bridge and begin walking. Yet how would he be able to focus on something on the other side, if he could not see it?

"Let go and start walking," a voice inside him said. As he stepped out, he could tell that the changes the cowboy made definitely improved things. The bridge seemed much firmer. Then he was in the middle and looking down; that old feeling rushed back. Again he was paralyzed. He tried to find something to focus on but still couldn't see the other side. He felt he had nowhere to go. He was suspended in the middle and could neither move nor breathe.

CHAPTER 11 *Focus and Alignment*

"Look inside and focus," Mitch heard a voice say. Was that coming from the cowboy again, or from inside of him? He closed his eyes and took a deep breath. The panic eased and Mitch felt a new calm as he began crossing once again.

When he reached the other side, Bill was sitting by a campfire, along with the cowboy. Bill said they were preparing for a meeting tomorrow with the tribal council, and invited Mitch to sit with them. The cowboy started a simple drumbeat and Bill followed. They motioned for Mitch to take up a drum and join them. He felt clumsy and out of sync with their beat. "Listen, Mr. Crandall, the beat is inside. Simply align yourself. Think together with us," the cowboy said softly. "Close your eyes and breathe, breathe with us." Then silence. Then there was just one sound, one beat of the drum, as they each played together. Clearly they were aligned.

As the drum beat faded, Bill asked Mitch what he was thinking as they were playing. "I was thinking about my college days at MIT, when I was part of a championship rowing team. We all started freshman year as a bunch of athletes looking for something to do, and tried scull racing. The first time out we ended up behind the starting line when the others had finished. It was quite embarrassing," he recalled ruefully.

"Being electrical engineers, we devised a unique system for practicing our strokes indoors by placing the racing scull on an electrical mat. We could tell when all of the oars touched the simulated water at exactly the same time and when they stroked the exact same length. We focused everything on rowing together with precisely the same power stroke. The goal was to keep everything in balance and become the most efficient team before returning to the water.

"When we reentered our first race at the intramural level our coxswain chanted in a steady rhythm, focus… together… focus… together… and none of us can remember what happened in that race. We weren't even aware of competition. We were simply focused on rowing together. We won, but didn't know when we'd crossed the finish line. It was truly effortless. We were all breathing together. We were all one." After a pause, he reflected, "It's been years since I've thought about that experience."

Then Bill silently got up and left the group, leaving his drum. The cowboy continued to play.

When Serving Others the Self-Image Disappears

"MR. CRANDALL, WHEN YOU ARE ALIGNED WITH OTHERS, you will feel one with nature. When you are serving others, your self-image disappears and the alignment appears. You become a part of something greater than just yourself. You are connected to everyone and them to you."

After a pause he said, "Life is about surrendering to what you want... to surrender to your dream. What is it that you want, Mr. Crandall? What is your dream?"

Mitch shut his eyes realizing that he had never answered that question before. He had always known what he wanted others to do and was very clear about what he did not want. That was easy. Determining what he wanted— that was a total shift. When he opened his eyes again, the cowboy had also disappeared.

Although he was alone, Mitch seemed to be connected with everyone he had ever known. He realized that was his dream...and it became totally real. He was no longer his image or position...but his dream....to be aligned with everyone in creating an inspired organization. That was what he wanted. He knew it from the moment he started working with the SynergyCorp team last week.

True Vision: Seeing Everyone and Everything Connected

ALONE BY THE CAMPFIRE, MITCH EXPERIENCED A RENEWED SPIRIT, much like he had felt playing in team sports. He recognized that he had felt that same spirit in 1980, when he watched the USA hockey team win the gold medal from Finland after beating the mighty, supposedly unbeatable Russian team the previous evening. "The entire country seemed to be a part of that team," he recalled out loud. "We were truly inspired." Had they, too, tapped into this aligned, energized space? he wondered. They obviously were focused on playing together instead of beating the Russians or the Finns, who clearly out-manned them in all aspects of the game.

Then Mitch remembered a time at the symphony when the musicians

and the audience became united; they became one. There was no separation. He was so inspired that he had the great conductor from the New York Philharmonic come speak to his management team. "I wanted him to get across how to bring out the best in people; how to have them all reach down inside and give their best; how to play in unison," he thought with disappointment. "It was received politely, but even with the maestro's help I didn't get the idea across to them.

"It's not likely an inspirational talk can achieve such a result," he thought. "Maybe it's only achieved by the things I'm experiencing here… being focused…playing in rhythm…being aligned around a vision. It's being able to see everyone as connected, working together and contributing. Just like SynergyCorp did for us. They were a part of us for those two days. They still are. They are somewhere deep inside of my very being and experience. I feel them there.

THEY WERE A PART OF US FOR THOSE TWO DAYS…
AND THEY STILL ARE. THEY ARE SOMEWHERE DEEP INSIDE OF
MY VERY BEING AND EXPERIENCE. I FEEL THEM THERE.

The Fundamental Choice: To Be Generative

"BILL SAID THAT IT TAKES A GENERATIVE ORGANIZATION TO CREATE inspired performance. (I'm glad he didn't say it takes generations!) That's my first fundamental choice — to clarify my focus and be generative; to share with others and allow others to share with me…to let them in… contributing ideas — their ideas. That's my vision, to align everyone around leverage points, with everyone fulfilling their purpose and achieving their dreams. All rowing together.

Feeling much like the designer of a ship ('the architect of the organization' that Bill had referred to), Mitch declared, "This is the beginning. It's the place that I must always come from. I will become a master of the generative context. It's my true self."

We All Want the Same Thing

MITCH CONTINUED HIS TRAIN OF THOUGHT FOR WHAT SEEMED LIKE JUST A MOMENT. Yet, when he looked up at the night sky, the stars were absolutely brilliant. As he stood up to stretch, he realized that his energy was connected to everything around him. He also realized that he had not eaten since brunch, and could smell a fire from the lodge. He left the drum where he had found it, alongside Bill's and the cowboy's.

Moving across the bridge, Mitch felt grounded in the dream he wanted to achieve. Stopping in the middle where the cowboy had done his repairs he was able to let go, look up, and draw energy from the stars above. The fear was gone, replaced with trust. He knew he no longer had to get people to do things. "We all want the same thing," he acknowledged with satisfaction, "to contribute — to make a difference. I don't have to get them to change or buy into this vision. It's who they are."

Entering the lodge, Mitch found the cowboy in the kitchen; he related that Bill was upstairs in his library. At the top of the stairs, Mitch stuck his head in the library door and asked if he could use Bill's phone for a couple of minutes. Rising from his chair, he replied, "Of course. I'll meet you downstairs for dinner."

Hesitating for a moment before dialing, Mitch reminded himself of his new grasp on relationships. All he could do was let someone in. "Well, he thought, it's worth a try." He listened nervously as the phone rang several times and was somewhat relieved when he finally got a voicemail. After the beep, he took a deep breath and softly said, "It's me…I know it's been far too long since we've spoken, and I deeply regret that. I want you to know that I love you and I am willing to do everything I can to make things right between us. It would mean the world to me to hear from you."

Mitch went to his room, cleaned up, and came down to dinner. The three men ate in silence. Nothing needed to be said. They were connected, not just with each other, but with everything.

CHAPTER 12 *Self Awareness, Self Reflection & Self Mangement*

T HE NEXT DAY MITCH WAS UP AT 6 AM AND COULD HEAR VOICES coming from downstairs. There were twelve people sitting around the fireplace. The cowboy was among them. Bill was there as well. There were long periods of silence and then one of them would speak. They were talking about their young people and the influence the world had on them. They spoke of the loss of values they were seeing in their youth. This was clearly the tribal council that Bill had mentioned.

Bill saw Mitch and motioned for him to come join them. As he came into the group, Mitch could see that the cowboy was recognized as a leader in their midst. They all paid him great homage, yet the cowboy was clearly the servant of them all… just as he had served Mitch completely during the past few days.

Mitch guessed they had been meeting for several hours because they were just concluding. It was clear what their mission was: they would work with each child to go on a vision quest in order to find his or her true self, as they called it. They needed to become grounded in the values of their people. Their nation depended on it. "We will lose our heritage and lose our youth if we fail on this mission." Resolve was written on the face of each member of the council. The commitment was to their destiny. Then they all stood, gathered their things, and left silently.

After they were gone, Bill said, 'Let's eat, Mitch, and then complete our discussions. I need to know your dream, so I can know how to serve you."

Over breakfast, Mitch related the experience from his walk, and later as he crossed the chasm. He revealed what he'd discovered about his dream. "My dream is for our organization to become Generative. My vision is to produce inspired performance. Bill, I was able to see everyone as contributors…generating and implementing ideas," he continued with unconcealed excitement.

Bill stated emphatically that he wanted to be a part of making Mitch's dream real, if he would let him. "Now I know how to serve you," he said with a warm smile. "Thank you. Without knowing your dream there is no real place to serve. This gives our relationship real purpose."

As Bill and Mitch settled at the conference table, the cowboy quietly joined them. Mitch began by asking eagerly, "What are the next steps?"

From Unconscious to Conscious

"FIRST," BILL REPLIED, "IT'S ESSENTIAL THAT EACH PERSON IN YOUR ORGANIZATION, much like the youth of the Indian nation, discover what motivates their behavior. They need to go on their own vision quest. They need to go from unconscious behavior to consciously making choices, each moment of their lives, based on their personal mission, values, principles and fundamental choices. They need to clarify their dreams and goals."

"That would be great," Mitch said with a chuckle, "but how will that happen short of a prefrontal lobotomy?"

Emotional Intelligence

"Mitch, it all starts with **emotional intelligence**, which comes from self-awareness, self-reflection and results in self-management. None of us can really manage others, nor does anyone truly want to be managed by others. We can only manage ourselves… and I still have trouble doing that," Bill admitted chuckling. "Best I can determine, most people have little control over what they put in their mouth, let alone what comes out of it when they speak. And eating and speaking are two areas of our lives over which we have absolute control. Basically, however, what we have control over are the choices we make. That's how we become responsible for our own behavior. We can really only manage being responsible."

"Ok, Bill, but how do we begin? Not everybody can come spend an evening in the sweat lodge, or sit around beating on drums," Mitch acknowledged contentedly.

"The one place to begin, no matter what we are exploring — whether it's your organization or yourself — is to discover the underlying structure that determines behavior. Remember, just as there's an underlying structure within organizations, there is also an underlying structure that determines how people behave.

"In the council, we talk about the paradoxical choices that each of us make. Armed with the combined knowledge of what we enjoy doing the most…and just as importantly, what we avoid, we can determine how we behave. Because the things we avoid tend to accumulate, they often consume our lives. They can end up having a snowball or domino effect similar to what we saw in your organization. In this sense, Mitch, every true choice is paradoxical in nature. We all live on the horns of a dilemma. Each moment in life, we have to choose one path over another. This is our personal reality. It's what determines our destiny."

> "ARMED WITH THE COMBINED KNOWLEDGE OF WHAT WE ENJOY DOING THE MOST . . . AND JUST AS IMPORTANTLY, WHAT WE AVOID, WE CAN DETERMINE HOW WE BEHAVE."

The Human Dilemma: Man's Human Nature vs. the Nature of Man

THE COWBOY FINALLY BROKE HIS SILENCE. "Mr. Crandall, man's 'human nature' dwells within each of us. It is all about survival. In most situations it is self-serving and functions only to protect one's self-image, which as you have discovered during your stay with us, doesn't even exist. It is fear-based and 'getting' in nature. It is totally reactive. When not required to save or protect your life when threatened, it functions to protect and defend the imagined concept each of us somehow created of ourselves. Because it is fear-based, what it projects onto the screen of the world and others is a reflection of itself. Therefore it projects fear, suspicion and distrust onto others or each situation that it encounters. When one believes that their self-image is who they are, everything they see must reinforce that image. Therefore what is seen is not real either. What you see is not what is actually happening, but rather a projection of where you come from. This becomes your context and determines all meaning in your life, resulting in fear-based and counter-productive behavior . . ."

Mitch interrupted, "Let me share with you the notes I made yesterday. I believe they closely reflect what you just shared. *Any event, person, or situation, whether real or imagined, is actually a projection of my self. The self-*

image is a circle of fear. What it sees (that which is threatening) doesn't actually exist, except in my mind. Therefore, most every situation that doesn't reinforce it is threatening. The situations that reinforce it — that prove me to be right — are themselves just defenses. Since this means that much of what I see does not actually exist — for heavens sake, what is real?"

The Power of the Unconscious Mind

"Don't get me wrong," mr. Crandall. "Your human nature is very real. It's a major part of your make-up. It is a big chunk of who you are, but it must be brought into a conscious world or it will become your silent dragon. Your mind is so powerful that it can create an imagined self, defend and protect it, and then create a world that reinforces it. That capability within us is very real. You see, we are all creators. Think about that. That is how powerful we actually are and how capable we can be. We can literally make things up and believe that they are real. Wisdom is being able to stand outside your self — we call it with a third eye, or the eagle's eye — and distinguish between what is real and what is not. You see, your self-image is just not the truth. When you can see that, and say it, then you are telling the truth about yourself. That is what sets you free. It is how you slay your dragon. You can create it and by telling the truth that you made it up, you set yourself free from it.

"Stay with me," he continued, noticing Mitch's look of puzzlement. "Imagine you had a cobra snake wrapped around your neck and it was all fanned out in front of your face, ready to strike at any moment. What would you do? Trying to get rid of it, it would strike you before you could even think about making a move. What if you tried to get away from it? Same outcome. What if you tried to kill it off? Well...you get the picture, I'm sure. Of all the options, none of them looks too good, except one that is unthinkable. You can disappear it."

Only the Truth Can Set You Free

"In our case, the self image is just that. It is your self-created cobra...the dragon within you. Anything other than telling the truth about it will only reinforce it and make it stronger and more dominant in your life. It will continuously cause your human nature to rule your life, thinking that survival is at stake in each situation that the ego perceives as threatening. When you are in survival you are unable to think clearly. In a sense, survival behavior is often what destroys you. So to dispel this myth called the self-image is to simply tell the truth about it. It is just made up. Since only the truth can set you free, when you tell the truth, whatever is not real will simply disappear. It was never real in the first place. If it were the truth it would set you free. Instead, you create your own prison in which you are the prisoner and the warden."

"So what is the truth"? Mitch asked, and then answered his own question. "Is it that we simply made up our self-image and have become its' prisoner? Is that it?" No one responded. The question just seemed to hang there. Then the cowboy continued.

The Nature of Man

"EQUALLY WITHIN US, THERE IS 'THE TRUE NATURE OF MAN.' It is our true nature to learn, develop, contribute, build, design, create and share. Our true nature is giving. All nature is in perfect balance. It is as Bill calls it: generative. It is a narrow path of living according to principles and laws of nature . . . and for me, at least, surrender to God. Others refer to the Universe or a Higher Power. That is a whole other discussion that we can have sometime, if you'd like.

"It is essential that we are aware at all times of these two dynamics within ourselves (Human Nature being Reactive and the Nature of Man being Generative) in order to consciously choose the right path. To choose to be Generative is our only choice."

"I can see," Mitch said thoughtfully after a pause, "how being reactive requires no real choice at all, just your built-in instincts to do what it takes to survive when you feel threatened or faced with anything that causes upset. It's the same for an out-of-balance condition in your life or organization." Mitch finished, realizing again that was how he had been functioning, both personally and as a CEO. He was reacting, even when he thought he was doing strategic planning or, as he called it, being strategic instead of tactical.

The Power of Alignment

AGAIN THE COWBOY SPOKE, "TO BE GENERATIVE ON A PERSONAL LEVEL, each person needs to come face to face with the choices they make. Especially those choices that have the greatest impact on their ability to perform at the highest level possible and make the greatest contribution. It is essential that we know the impact we have on others. We need to recognize our differences, yet know how to align with others to create a team and build an organization that can grow in a balanced manner over time. That is the power of alignment.

"We are all uniquely different. By contributing to others we become a part of them. We let others in by serving them. It is only then that we are fulfilling our purpose…the reason for which we exist.

"Life choices are determined by many things. In the council we always start with how a person views the world and how they believe things are going to turn out in the future. We want to know, do they deeply value the ideas of others or do they only care about what they think? Ultimately, we think it is essential to be grounded in all areas that influence the quality of decisions one makes and how a person goes about implementing them."

"TO BE GENERATIVE ON A PERSONAL LEVEL, EACH PERSON NEEDS TO COME FACE TO FACE WITH THE CHOICES THEY MAKE."

"But, in business, how is it possible to gain this level of self-awareness? How do we determine these aspects of ourselves so that we can make conscious choices? Keep in mind, I hire people to make sales, to engineer and produce products; I have to make payroll every two weeks."

Taking a Vision Quest is facing Life's Paradoxical Choices

"MR. CRANDALL, IF YOU WILL ALLOW ME, I WOULD LIKE TO TAKE YOU ON A JOURNEY and tell you the story of a young brave and what he faced as he went on his personal vision quest. In reality, however, it is what each of us faces on a daily basis as we choose between our human nature and the nature of man. It is what determines whether one is reactive or generative. It determines the degree of contribution one makes or how much of a contradiction one becomes throughout life. It is why some people have satisfaction in their work and lives and others suffer."

"While you do," Bill interjected, rising from the conference table, "I'm going to excuse myself to handle some personal business. I'll see you in a bit."

As Bill went up to his library, the cowboy began his story.

"During a vision quest a brave must come face to face with each dimension of the self. If any one aspect is out of balance, it will have a very strong influence on other dimensions of behavior. Imbalances — when unconscious — act as an automatic program in the brain. They cause reinforcing actions from others and the environment. They produce rigidity and limit one's personal and organizational effectiveness and ability to serve.

"Just as there is an eco-system that maintains a constant state of balance in nature, there is also one that operates psychologically, in our minds. When someone is paradoxically out of balance in one area of their life, we often say 'the rabbits are getting out of control again.' Let me explain.

"This is a not just a good story, it actually happens every three years or so, right here on our tribal lands. But similar stories exist everywhere, if you look in nature.

"About every three years we will have a period of rain. This causes the food source for rabbits to become plentiful; of course this attracts more rabbits. You know what rabbits do best when they get together. They multiply. As they grow in number it causes a multiplier effect and they begin to expand exponentially. Suddenly, there are rabbits having a great time everywhere." Mitch smiled appreciatively.

"But after a period of great consumption and reproduction, they deplete the food source and there is less food per rabbit. Some become weaker and others stronger, with the stronger rabbits now getting the majority of the food.

"Of course when there are lots of rabbits, this attracts their natural predator, the fox. As foxes arrive on the scene, some rabbits are weaker due to less food per rabbit. The foxes are able to easily feast on them, thus attracting more fellow foxes. The word gets out and the rabbit population is living in fear of the foxes. The period of rain has passed and the food source is drying up, resulting in less food per rabbit and more foxes feasting on this weakened condition. Soon the rabbit population is diminished and the foxes move on, seeking better hunting grounds."

Relating his story to their previous conversation, the cowboy pointed out that we all have these imbalances that affect us, but don't know that is what's limiting our ability to perform as well as we know we're able to. "That's why it is essential to make conscious choices. It leads to self-management. When a person takes disciplined action based on awareness," he went on to explain, "the imbalance acts like a personal leverage point — resulting in one's being able to significantly expand their contribution and diminish their contradictory nature."

After some reflection, Mitch said, "In other words, just like your greatest strength can become your greatest weakness, when aware, your greatest weaknesses have the ability to become your greatest strengths. They can become your personal leverage points."

"That is another way of putting it, Mr. Crandall."

"Your example sounds like the situation we're facing in our industry right now. All of those conditions exist. That was revealed by the underlying structure and time histories of my business that we mapped out yesterday.

154

Our suppliers are drying up. The money source that was once abundant is depleted. The foreign competitors and investors are taking advantage of the weakened condition of companies in the industry. I guess the rabbits are out of control and the foxes are feasting," Mitch concluded wryly.

The Psychological Eco-Structure

"EXACTLY, MR. CRANDALL. IT IS ALSO TRUE WITHIN EACH OF US AS WELL. Since we each have an internal psychological eco-structure, if there are areas that are out of balance, and they go unconsciously unchecked, they can rigidly dominate our behavior. This obviously causes upset conditions and limits our growth. These imbalances act like a thief in the night, robbing us of personal satisfaction and fulfillment. Only in this case, the thief is within ourselves and we do not even know we have been violated.

"On a vision quest each brave must visit the paradoxes within himself. He must also be willing to be vulnerable. This is true for all of us. It is essential that these paradoxes become known in order to maximize one's contribution to others, their tribe or organization, and indeed the world they live in. As each paradox is addressed, a person must seek to develop and balance that aspect of the self in order to experience satisfaction in each area of life.

> "ON A VISION QUEST EACH BRAVE MUST VISIT THE
> PARADOXES WITHIN HIMSELF. HE MUST ALSO BE WILLING TO
> BE VULNERABLE. THIS IS TRUE FOR ALL OF US."

Slaying the Dragon Within

"IT IS OUR MISSION THROUGHOUT LIFE TO CONTINUOUSLY EXPAND our effectiveness by going beyond our self-imposed limitations. My people call it slaying the dragon within one's self. It is an internal battle for one's freedom from self-interests and human nature. It is making a shift from protecting the self-image to living consciously, based on fundamental choices. This is what determines a person's destiny. We believe it is what will determine the very future of our nation. It is about the survival and the future of our people. It is about yours, Bill's and my destiny."

Both sat spellbound by the power of what they had just shared.

Then Mitch broke the silence (as he now recognized he tended to do — but couldn't help himself; the silence seemed to get to him) and asked, "You mentioned outlook. Is that like context? Is that where this begins?"

"Yes it is, Mr. Crandall. Your context defines your outlook and gives meaning to everything around you. It is that which determines your world.

"But first, let me tell you the story of the vision quest I mentioned. One of our brightest braves left the tribal lands to attend Harvard University. The tribe, along with scholarships, both academic and athletic, and his willingness to work, financed his way through school. He worked hard. He excelled and was offered a job on Wall Street. He prospered there, but became very self-indulgent. He became consumed with work and gaining stature. He became full of himself and forgot his roots. These were good times on Wall Street. People were making big money and companies with little value were experiencing incredible stock growth, even though they were often not profitable. It was a crazy time.

"Then almost overnight people recognized that these companies were not just overvalued, they had no real value, and the market collapsed. A fortune of investor capital was lost — trillions of dollars — along with the brave's investor's money.

"The young brave had led people into investments without fully analyzing the risks and informing them of the downsides of their investments. Indeed, he did not see them himself. He was certain of his own opinions and beliefs, and had not been open to feedback, clear warning signs, or the ideas of others. He was impulsive and authoritative. He was not a good steward of other people's money or their trust in him.

"Sadly, he was not aware of these things about himself. He thought he was serving others by making them wealthy in the stock market. Only later did he recognize that he was driven — not by serving others — but by his desire for money and recognition. Because his motivation and enthusiasm were contagious and he had superb communications skills, people believed in him. They trusted him. They encouraged their friends to invest with him. They liked him. He was warm and empathic. No one knew, not even himself, where he was taking them or why. He was a leader who believed in himself. He was confident and cocky with charisma.

"As he grew up and became successful, everyone in the tribe felt he was their future leader. But now, even though he had become extremely wealthy, he was disgraced and was a disgrace to his people. He had to come face to face with the dragon within himself: his own lack of awareness of his personal desires and imbalances."

As the cowboy spoke, Mitch sensed deep emotion emanating from him. At that moment he intuitively knew the cowboy was sharing his own story, his own personal tragedy, his own rediscovery of his true self.

"The brave returned to his people and told his story. The wise men of the tribal council, each representing one of twelve paradoxes that determine ones behavior, began a systematic process of revealing the choices that he had made and how they caused him to take a self-serving path that led to his sorrow and suffering."

"HE WAS CERTAIN OF HIS OWN OPINIONS AND BELIEFS, AND HAD NOT BEEN OPEN TO FEEDBACK, CLEAR WARNING SIGNS, OR THE IDEAS OF OTHERS. HE WAS IMPULSIVE AND AUTHORITATIVE."

Mitch took a deep breath and released it slowly. He was thinking about himself and his own way of behaving.

"First, they said, his downfall was guided by his self-image and unconscious imbalances. His self-created dragon ruled him. One painful step at a time, he must slay his dragon.

"As he began to take charge of his life again, he came to realize that — unbeknownst to him — he had always been on his vision quest. Over time, he developed the ability to observe himself, moment to moment, as he actually was. He overcame his personal blindness. He began to make conscious choices. He finally began to truly serve others. He began to lead by serving."

Self Reflection

NOT WANTING TO INTERRUPT, MITCH HESITATED TO SPEAK. Quietly he thought to himself, "I, too, have been on my vision quest." He was flooded with emotion, knowing that so much of his life was blind to this level of seeing and personal understanding. "What a waste." he thought. "Where did I go wrong?"

Gaining the courage to speak, Mitch admitted, "In my own way I, too, have sought foremost to get ahead, to dominate the industry and to gain recognition. It never resulted in satisfaction or fulfillment," he acknowledged sadly.

Unable to speak further, Mitch's thoughts and feelings became a jumble: was his ambition just a cover-up of his own fears? Was he trying to fill the empty place he often felt within himself? Then it struck him. There were areas of his life that were completely unfulfilling; areas where he never experienced the level of satisfaction that he should have, given all he had accomplished. He was so self-critical that no matter what recognition he received, he didn't believe it or trust that it was real.

"IN MY OWN WAY I, TOO, HAVE SOUGHT FOREMOST TO GET AHEAD, TO DOMINATE THE INDUSTRY AND GAIN RECOGNITION. IT NEVER RESULTED IN SATISFACTION OR FULFILLMENT."

His communications were always blunt and to the point. He thought he was just a person "who always lays things on the line," as he proudly told people. Had he simply rationalized all of his own imbalances? Where the brave was impulsive, he was a strict disciplinarian about analyzing everything. He was always digging into the reasons another person's ideas would not work, priding himself on discovering the flaws and lack of detail in strategies that would defeat others in a debate. He excelled in debate both in high school and college. He was passionate about it. Now he knew why. Even in his Executive MBA, he strived to outdo the executives from other companies. He felt his image was at stake. He even felt driven to outdo his teammates when they did case studies. Where would it end?

Mitch could see how he lacked the warmth the cowboy had. He lacked his caring and helpful spirit. He was often harsh in his evaluation, judgment and supervision of others. He and the cowboy were so different; yet, so much the same.

Mitch knew he, too, had to understand the paradoxical choices that caused this rigid way of addressing many of the critical things he did. All of a sudden, his chest tightened, and he could not breathe again. "What is it I don't know about myself that's restricting my effectiveness?" he thought in quiet desperation. "After all I've been through this weekend it's still a mystery to me. I did an intensive self-assessment process years ago — yet nothing I did really gave me insight into my more unconscious choices. Even though I went through the Outward Bound three-year program to challenge my limits and take me to what they called 'the higher ground,' I still feel limited and stuck in how I respond emotionally. Now I'm uncertain whether my decisions are delivering the right message to my people; my behavior is not producing the desired results."

Yet somehow, Mitch knew that what he was going through as the cowboy spoke was completely different from Outward Bound. Outward Bound was easy for him. It was dealing with physical and mental challenges. He loved that kind of stuff and always took to it with great enthusiasm, just as he equally was always seeking the next mountain to climb inside the business. He called it "the courage to take initiative and challenges." For him, life was about overcoming obstacles and achieving goals.

Then once again it hit Mitch in the face — he was always overcoming difficulties. But what was wrong with that? Perhaps nothing. Yet perhaps it was that perspective that had influenced some of the decisions he made that placed the company in jeopardy. He also knew he evaluated his management team based on what he valued doing himself. "Just like the brave, I am dominated and consumed by my own dragons, but couldn't see them until now," he admitted sadly. Surely that had caused him to be judgmental towards his son John, who had none of his own characteristics. No doubt that is why he was drawn to Mark, who was so much like him.

Mitch knew that the insight and view he needed now was of his inner vision. He felt that once he could see the place he saw others from, he could finally see himself (and them) with real clarity. He thought he needed to start by addressing everything he knew was driven from his inner self — his fears and self-serving needs. These had most certainly determined the impact and kind of influence he had had on others. He had to go from being Outward

Bound to Inward.

Historically, Mitch viewed the organization's growth as just another personal mountain to climb. Yet he never seemed satisfied with his results or that of others. "Maybe all I see around me is really a projection of my self, just as Bill said. In that case, all my beliefs, perceptions and judgments about others are simply a reflection of me. No wonder I see what I see that others don't see, or seem unable to see. What is it that they do see? I guess I've never sought to truly understand them or myself. I just wanted to win. I wanted to dominate…defend…protect…gain…achieve…."

The cowboy interrupted Mitch's thoughts as he continued his story.

"In order to set the brave on his path of discovery, the first member of the council spoke to him about his outlook. He said it was necessary to have absolute clarity about his beliefs and opinions along with a willingness to be open to viewpoints from others. 'When you hear others' ideas, do you truly reflect on them as having equal or greater value than your own?' he was challenged. He knew he did not.

'Are you one who seeks to know the truth…or are you one who simply judges others' ideas based on your own opinions and closely-held beliefs? Beware,' he was warned, 'that the strength of your beliefs do not lead to being dogmatic and uncompromising. When you are quite strong in your opinions,' he was told, 'you limit what you can hear from others; it causes you to only be able to associate with those who agree with you.'

"This was very true of the young brave. He was headstrong in this manner. He was clearly dogmatic in his views. This led to his not seeking the truth. The place that he viewed the world from was narrow and limiting. He needed to shift his strong beliefs to a commitment to knowing and discovering the truth, not proving himself right. He needed to become more like a scientist, who seeks to prove himself wrong in pursuit of the truth.

"The master teacher who led the vision quests said that inside each of us there are paradoxes. Each paradox, he said, had a dynamic side and a gentle side, much like the male and female, or the light and dark of life. To become balanced, one needs to develop both sides of each paradox.

"He taught that if you are overly strong in a dynamic trait, like being certain of yourself, your opinions and beliefs, you need to create balance

by developing your gentle side. To not seek that balance l
forms of self-inflicted suffering. The balance for certain
being able to reflect on and be open to many different vi
develops your gentle side and moves you closer to discovering the truth.

"Then the teacher gave the brave a parable to consider: 'There was a
man who was so strong that others became dependent on him. He had
strong opinions and was seen as courageous. Others trusted him. He
became a leader and was thought to be invulnerable. But he only followed his own advice. He became deaf to the wisdom of the world, to the
laws of nature and the principles of life, and lost his way…all the while
thinking he was sure of everything. Every time he thought he was heading
upward and achieving personal goals, he was only digging his way out of a
self-created hole.'"

"ARE YOU ONE WHO SEEKS TO KNOW THE TRUTH… OR ARE
YOU ONE WHO SIMPLY JUDGES OTHERS' IDEAS BASED ON
YOUR OWN OPINIONS AND CLOSELY HELD BELIEFS?"

The Root of Ignorance and the Source of Conflict

"ANOTHER COUNCIL MEMBER EXPLAINED, 'THE ROOT OF IGNORANCE EXISTS when
proving others wrong and making yourself right. It separates you from others. It disconnects you from the energy that is only present when you are
connected with those around you. When you are disconnected, energy is
drained; communication becomes a "duo log," much like two TV sets talking.
Assumptions are made, resulting in conflict and upsets.'

"As he let this in, the brave recognized his need to always be superior. He
had become the master of his own rightness."

As Mitch listened, he saw his own need to feel superior and prove he was
right, which meant that someone else would always end up being wrong.

Seek and Serve the Truth

"ANOTHER WISE ONE SPOKE TO THE BRAVE. 'The objective of life is to seek to
know and serve the truth. Pursuing one's personal happiness is often driven

avoiding unhappiness or seeking pleasure. Happiness is often illusionary and based on outside conditions — or others. Like you, all men are the cause of what exists in their lives. They are the cause of their happiness. They are the cause of their own downfall. No one else is to blame.'

"As the wise one continued, the brave could grasp that wisdom comes from understanding the motives and ideas of others; but that level of wisdom is found deep within oneself. For only when you know yourself can you possibly be connected with, know and understand or experience others. When you experience others at this level, you finally experience yourself.

"When the council session ended, the brave was asked to reflect deeply on all he had heard. They would meet again."

Looking intently at the cowboy, Mitch knew that this was also his own story.

Finding Balance in All Things

"EACH TIME THEY MET, THE COUNCIL PROVIDED THE BRAVE support and feedback. They dealt with the remainder of the paradoxes that determined both his balances and imbalance. Each paradox revealed his way of behaving and making decisions that had been hidden from himself.

"He discovered he had much to consider. He was extremely optimistic about his ability to influence how the future was going to turn out. What limited him was his unwillingness to explore hard data and to dig beneath the surface to discover what could go wrong in his approach to things. For his own point of view about things distorted his world. It blinded him from seeing what was plainly and directly in front of him. There was blindness to his optimism. His way of operating led him to make decisions that did not benefit those who had entrusted their investments to his care. He was not a worthy steward of other's trust in him. He tended to not take their input seriously. All this — plus his impulsiveness and willingness to take risks without due diligence or consideration of the ways of nature — exacerbated his lack of responsibility.

"He ultimately came to see how he had failed those who trusted him. He was confronted by his lack of vision, his inability to see, his blindness and his point of view. He was blinded by his own deficit-driven needs and desires to achieve, to look good, to get more, indeed, be more."

After a moment of reflection, the cowboy continued. "The council was very directive in the developmental actions they asked of him. He was given parables to consider. He was required to meet head-on the consequences of his irresponsible actions and the impact they had on others.

"Thus the brave began to face everyone who had placed trust in him. It was then that he personally experienced the upset and suffering he had caused. No longer was he able to avoid his consequences. As all things do, his actions had come full circle. He experienced their suffering as his own.

"Then the brave was given another parable to reflect on. He carries it on his person for daily council."

Mitch watched spellbound as the cowboy reached into his wallet, pulled out a tattered paper and began to read. Mitch recognized that it was biblically based.

There were three servants who were entrusted with talents by their master. One invested the money for personal gain without a long-term focus or without deep thought. The second was fearful and buried the money, hoping that he would be proved right in his skepticism. The third sought out the council of others, sought to understand and master the theory behind investing, explored all the risks involved and in due time invested slowly, with great care, based on principles, ancient wisdom and a sense of stewardship.

He was rewarded by a life of abundance for himself and others.

The other two were sent away in shame, humbled before others. For they were both foolish.

Carefully, the cowboy returned the paper to his wallet before continuing. "Likewise, here was a brave who had been given many great gifts of the Spirit. He was blessed with an ability to connect with others and was passionate and convincing about what they should do. In this area of his life he experienced personal satisfaction. He loved it when people would buy his services and when he could see them place their trust in him. But they, too, were driven by greed and the desire to make a big score. When they expressed their desires to him he encouraged them and played off their human nature. His strengths attracted more and more people to him and he developed deeply personal, trusting relationships.

"However, the power that is wielded by having the gift of great communication skills carries even greater — times ten — personal responsibility with it. Now he had to return to those people to whom he had convincingly sold his investment strategies and whose money he had lost. He had to intervene with them to release them from their past experience with him, as they had become bitter and fearful. They were resentful and felt betrayed. Many wanted revenge. They had trusted him; now they were full of distrust. 'They had felt that it was different with him. It was not just investing in the market and taking their chances. They had invested in him.'

Communication Means being One with Another

"THE ELDEST OF THE COUNCIL HAD BEEN SILENT. HE FINALLY SPOKE. 'All action that is taken must be done so in a true partnership. Whatever action or decision is taken in the present must be viewed as being forever. When one communicates, one enters into communion with the other person. It is not something you do to another; it is what you become with the other person. You become them. To communicate is to become one with another.'

"What he then said hit the young brave like a lightening bolt. 'For what you have done to others, we too must bear the burden. We, the members of the council, are equally responsible for the actions of our people. What you have done to others, we have done to them as well.

'You must walk in the other person's moccasins, carrying his burden as your own, all the while knowing that the decisions they make must be their own...not yours through persuasion. This is true communication.'

Violating the Laws of Nature

"ONLY THEN COULD THE BRAVE SEE THAT HE HAD NOT ONLY VIOLATED THE LAWS of nature, but had violated his very roots. He had planted foolishly in the late fall expecting a full harvest. He had failed to work with the forces of nature; indeed, the forces of change. He trusted only in himself, not in the ways of nature, the ways of true change. He had relied on his strength to communicate. His strengths had become his weaknesses. His talents had become his liabilities. He was reminded that 'To whom much is given... much is required.'

"Yet, on the other hand, his great communication skills were coupled with a naturally helpful spirit. There was nothing he would not do for others and they felt this to be true about him. As is often the case on Wall Street, he was not just looking out for himself — for number one. What made his offerings so compelling is that people actually felt he cared deeply about them; indeed he believed he did, for he enjoyed assisting others. It gave him great pleasure.

" . . . THE POWER THAT IS WIELDED BY HAVING THE GIFT OF GREAT COMMUNICATION SKILLS CARRIES EVEN GREATER — TIMES TEN — PERSONAL RESPONSIBILITY WITH IT."

"The irony of it all, when one thinks deeply on these things, is that the brave had a great heart for others. His powerful communications skills were coupled with warmth, caring, and an empathic manner. Yet with all of his strengths he lacked the personal decision-making capacity to handle peoples' resources. In reality he lacked personal integrity, but without knowing it or even understanding why."

Mitch could hear the cowboys' voice crack and saw his lips quiver as he abruptly concluded this statement. He knew the cowboy felt this deeply.

Mitch was also deep in thought. "How different we are. I have good analytical skills and decision-making ability, but am lacking the cowboy's warmth, caring and communication skills." Listening to the cowboy was like holding up a mirror for him to see himself with a new level of clarity.

Self-Management: Using Strengths to Develop Weaknesses

HE RECOGNIZED THAT HE NEEDED TO DEVELOP WHAT THE COWBOY naturally had and that the cowboy had needed to develop what he seemed to naturally possess. "But how do I go about this development process?" he wondered.

Then it hit him. The answer was right in front of him. This was like crossing the chasm. He needed to focus his attention on those specific areas within himself. He needed, as the cowboy had said when he was stuck in the middle of the bridge, 'to look within.' Those areas of development were his personal leverage points. He needed to go to the middle of his own bridge and strengthen it where he was weakest. He needed to use his strengths to develop his weaknesses.

What some did naturally, Mitch realized, he needed to focus on and develop. This would require mastering certain principles through discipline and self-management. This would require clarity and focus, consciously placing his attention and taking action with commitment and intention. This was his bridge to cross — and strengthen.

"What are my strengths and weakness?" he asked himself. "I certainly am strongly driven, and both want and seek challenge. I'm excellent at strategic decision-making and analyzing things. I hold people accountable. But I'm blunt in my communications and harsh in my evaluation of others. Now I need to find my own brave inside of me." Again, his life flooded before him, allowing him to see the impact of his own rigid imbalances, just as the cowboy had shared his while telling the story of the brave.

Then the cowboy stood and slowly pulled on a chain that ran into his pocket. Out came his watch. Mitch noticed that he wound it slowly and caringly, with what seemed like warmth and affection. "Everything he does has caring written all over it," Mitch thought with wonder. "He served me caringly all weekend, yet he is the undisputed leader of his Indian nation."

"Mr. Crandall, I need to get you back to the airport if you are going to catch your plane on time. Let me leave you with Bill for a while, so that you can plan out your next steps. I will meet you across the bridge, and have the horse saddled. I will accompany you part of the way back to your plane, and someone will tend your horse when you get there. Thank you for allowing me to share this story."

166

CHAPTER 13 *Building a Generative Organizatio and Achieving Inspired Performance*

After the cowboy left, Bill joined Mitch and the two men sat in reflective silence. "How," Mitch asked, turning to Bill with a shake of his head, "do we achieve this level of self-awareness and management in our company?"

Predictive Assessment Based on the Twelve Paradoxes

"MITCH, I DID A WORLD-WIDE SEARCH LOOKING FOR AN ASSESSMENT INSTRUMENT that would reveal to a person the choices that determine their behavior. I wanted something that would be predictive in nature and would allow an individual, myself, or you as an executive, to predict how a person was going to behave in specific situations. What would they do under stress? What was their dark or subconscious level of thinking that determined their behavior? If they could be made aware of it, I believed, it would allow them to make choices and take action to bring about change and personal effectiveness. After three years we found nothing that would meet our standards.

> "I WANTED SOMETHING THAT WOULD BE PREDICTIVE IN
> NATURE AND WOULD ALLOW AN INDIVIDUAL . . . .
> TO PREDICT HOW A PERSON WAS GOING TO BEHAVE
> IN SPECIFIC SITUATIONS."

"Thanks to SynergyCorp I was introduced to the Harrison Assessment (HA). It is based on the idea that what you enjoy, you will do more often and without supervision. You will seek to improve performance and receive positive feedback. Equally, what you don't enjoy you put off or avoid and only do it under the duress of supervision. Almost all supervisory time is taken up by addressing what people avoid or do not get better at."

"The unique thing about the HA is that it's based on the paradoxes people

performance. People who've been able to resolve within
ingly contradictory paradoxical choices are able to perform
levels."

"How many paradoxes are there?" Mitch asked. "There must be hundreds of paradoxes; most of them wouldn't have anything to do with performance inside a company, would they?"

"Basically there are twelve paradoxes that seem to affect performance areas like leadership effectiveness, managerial discipline, customer service, sales ability, project implementation, the ability to execute strategically versus tactically, and so forth. Each of them, however, combines with one another in very powerful ways. By using the results from the assessment we're able to achieve a high level of self-awareness and reflection that results in self-management. If we're going to be able to go from reactive behavior to inspired performance, it's essential that we achieve a very high level of self-awareness.

"Just as we'll map out the underlying structure of your organization with your management team, each person in your organization will be able to graph out their paradoxical choices. From that, a personal development plan can transform negative areas impacting the organization into their highest-leverage points for personal and organizational effectiveness. In fact, Mitch, SynergyCorp uses the Harrison Assessment as the basis for their entire selection, promotion and development process. It allows them to find the ideal match between a person and the job. It sure made my job easy when we put together the supplier management program."

"I look forward to doing that. Before I leave, Bill, give me a thumbnail outline of what else is going to be required."

Six Strategies and Six Managerial Disciplines

"As you will recall, fundamentally, there are six areas of strategic focus. We discussed these yesterday and your assessment results revealed where you are in each one of them. We spent time yesterday on just one, Sales Effectiveness. The other five need to be addressed just as we did your sales issues. When we finish you will have time histories and feedback loops on Leadership Effectiveness, Customer Enthusiasm, Employee Inspiration,

Productive Capacity and Competitive Advantage Creation.

"Your ability to execute each strategy requires discipline in Performance Management, Process Management, Learning and Knowledge Management, Project Management and Change Management.

Where we will begin is in performance management, which starts with clarity of focus and building trust on an individual-by-individual basis — just like we did with the Plywood plant.

Clarity of Purpose

"As you must realize by now, it's essential to have absolute clarity in all aspects of your organization. Knowing how you run the company, Mitch, you're excellent in this area. I had to really struggle with it when I first began. People didn't know what the playing field was like. This allowed them to operate without knowledge of boundaries or having well-defined personal and organizational mission statements. My agreements with people were based on assumptions, not clearly defined ways of operating and expectation statements. We also lacked performance standards that were based on actual results. Only later did I discover the power of Purpose. Without clarity of purpose, alignment is virtually impossible. That kind of clarity is all defining.

"Since then, I've created a model that provides the elements required to build a Generative Organization and achieve inspired performance. It's based on what we discovered was limiting growth and causing upset conditions. It reveals what it takes for everyone to go beyond their best performance on a daily basis. Since developing the basic model, we now customize it for each organization, fitting it into their dynamics and initiatives. This provides constant feedback and allows them to know at all times where they stand."

Bill handed Mitch a model that outlined the dimensions of what inspired performance would look like. He explained that he'd like to hold onto it for now; he preferred each organization he worked with to draw its own model and determine the way it looked so it was their vision, not his.

Making Fundamental Choices

"The next challenge we had was working with every person in the company so they could clearly state their dream and the fundamental choices they needed to make to have it be real."

"I think mine might be 'to do what it takes to build a Generative Organization; to shift from reacting to events; to work with the underlying structure focused on changing our behavior patterns over time.' How's that for being a good student?" Mitch asked happily.

"... TO DO WHAT IT TAKES TO BUILD A GENERATIVE ORGANIZATION; TO SHIFT FROM REACTING TO EVENTS; TO WORK WITH THE UNDERLYING STRUCTURE FOCUSED ON CHANGING OUR BEHAVIOR PATTERNS OVER TIME."

The Pathway

"IT'S ABSOLUTELY WONDERFUL, MITCH. ONCE YOU MAKE A FUNDAMENTAL CHOICE, all the principles that you must follow show up. They become more than signs pointing you in the direction you must go; they are the pathway. What you need to focus on and where you need to place your attention to achieve the right amount of movement becomes clear. If you violate them and fall off the path, you — and everyone else — suffers. If you follow them you will achieve an optimum rate of growth. You will maintain your balance through focused momentum."

Individual Commitment is based on Mission, Purpose, and a Dream

"SO EVERY PERSON HAS A DEFINED DREAM AND PURPOSE," Mitch clarified, rising and moving to the expansive window. "Every person has a mission statement committed to certain ways of behaving. I did that on my Outward Bound experience and we incorporated it into the GT Leadership Academy. Yet I've never established the policy in my own company. I guess this is where the rubber meets the road. I'd like to dedicate our efforts to having everyone develop this level of commitment," he concluded, turning to face Bill.

"As you know, Bill, I'm a long-time runner. I go out every evening about five or six o'clock with good intentions. There's a juncture that I come to as I'm struggling to get up a rather steep hill in my neighborhood. If I make the choice to go right, I'm just another half mile from my home and it's all down hill. I will have run two miles, which is okay I guess. But if I take a turn to another hill, and then I'm on a path that results in about a four. At about the three-mile marker — I guess the endorphins kick ning becomes effortless. I feel like my life is on target and I become energized. The level of satisfaction increases the further I run. When I finally get home I'm exhilarated. I have great satisfaction.

"However, when I take the path to the right, the short cut, if you will, I'm exhausted when I reach the house. I'm out of breath and there's no real enjoyment from the run. I think that's what you mean. You become 'the path' or 'the way' you take. It's actually who you are. 'The path' is living by those three insights, starting with all things are energy which takes the path of least resistance. We're only able to change it by changing the underlying structure and following a few principles…as you shared with me when we began." Pausing thoughtfully and looking Bill directly in the eyes, Mitch concluded, "Everything we're talking about, it's actually just a place inside you, isn't it?"

Again there was silence. Bill smiled, but did not answer.

" . . . YOU BECOME 'THE PATH' OR 'THE WAY' YOU TAKE.
IT'S ACTUALLY WHO YOU ARE."

Moving back to the table, Mitch broke the silence once again. "One other thing bothers me, though. What about goal setting for achievement? Shouldn't our people have goals? Isn't goal achievement essential? I've lived and breathed them my whole life."

Every Person a Goal Setter and Goal Achiever

"Of course. That is the real job of a manager. In building a generative organization and creating inspired performance, every person ultimately becomes a goal setter and goal achiever. We'll set up a scorecard that charts how well each manager is developing every person in meeting their goals. The ultimate goal that each person achieves is to daily go beyond their past best performance. There are very specific steps to facilitating that process, but it's not brain surgery, believe me. Yet they don't exist within most organizational settings. Where they do, it leads to inspired performance."

"Great. That really seems to resonate with me. The idea of every person being a goal setter and a goal achiever is inspiring. But like you say, it rarely exists. I guess in a reactive organization, even if every person did have goals, they'd quickly get disillusioned, become frustrated and go back to fire fighting."

"Even though fire fighting often results in goal setting, it's is out of a reactive state — not a generative orientation," Bill affirmed.

Scorekeeping for Inspired Performance

"THEN HOW DO YOU MAINTAIN A GENERATIVE STATE?"

"Glad you asked, because, despite the value of everything we've worked on up to now, when it comes down to building an inspired workforce, it's somehow directly related to establishing a scorekeeping system that results in self management. Without it no one really knows whether they're winning or not. If you don't know if you're winning, you can't really win. So why try? Then people start working for a paycheck instead of achieving their dream… or accomplishing what they previously thought to be impossible. That's what really inspires people."

"Bill, this sounds a lot like good old fashioned performance management," Mitch said doubtfully. "We have performance measures and KRA's. We measure every area of productivity and results, but it doesn't inspire people. Now that I think about it, it often causes this 'human nature' to kick in and everyone starts covering themselves and protecting their budgets. I don't know, Bill. I question if scorekeeping will lead to inspiration. I sure haven't seen it happen in my organization."

"What you say is true, Mitch, absolutely. No one wants to be measured or evaluated by someone else called a manager. It causes them to look out for number one. Those kinds of measures can and do destroy teamwork and alignment. They'll suppress energy and connectedness and often cause fear in people.

"The Scorekeeping for Inspired Performance process transforms all of this fear-based behavior into shared energy. Remember, all things are energy, and energy cannot be created or destroyed — only released or suppressed. The scorekeeping we'll engage in is designed to release energy. It's based on each person's contribution toward fulfilling their dream.

172

It becomes an essential part of the underlying structure. It's right at the core of the organization. It's how to maintain clarity of focus and alignment around your highest leverage points. It's the very basis of achieving an optimum rate of growth, both personally and organizationally."

Productivity and Production Capacity
"BUT WHAT ABOUT PRODUCTIVITY? WON'T WE LOSE OUR FOCUS ON RESULTS?"

"Mitch, there are two parts to productivity that this process focuses on. The first is focus on actual results. Productivity will be charted over time so that each person knows how they're doing by the end of each day. Ideally, we found that when keeping score they should know almost moment-to-moment how they're doing — just like in a sporting event or a game that they're playing. We want to set up the entire workforce so they can play to win when winning is defined as going beyond their best past performance.

Competency Development and Organizational Learning
"THE OTHER FOCUS IS ON DEVELOPING THE PRODUCTIVE CAPACITY OF EACH PERSON, and therefore, that of the entire organization. All development is self-development. The real business you're in is constantly increasing the developmental competencies of the organization. That must become your core foundation and focus.

"Management's capability to constantly increase personal and organizational competencies and production capacity is what ultimately contributes to consistently higher levels of performance and productivity. This requires the development of individual and organizational learning strategies, which is the purpose of my organization. Our mission is the implementation of strategies for optimum growth. That's what we are all about. It's an orientation, not just a vision statement on the wall."

Idea Generation and Personal Contribution
BILL WENT ON TO EXPLAIN HOW, IN A TRULY GENERATIVE ORGANIZATION, the ultimate measure of productivity is the number of new ideas implemented per person each month. The bottom line effect is to reduce costs and cycle time while improving quality, service and individual involvement. Idea genera-

tion and contribution is what inspired performance is all about.

"That's when we see people achieve an entirely different level of performance. That's when self-management takes over. It's in people seeing their ideas implemented and being recognized for their contribution. That's when and how they become a part of, connected to, something bigger than themselves."

Mitch stood for a stretch, feeling a bit overwhelmed with the task before him, when Bill asked, "Mitch, do you remember visiting my plant, and I showed you our wall of inspired performers? We had photos of people along with their ideas that had improved various conditions, either in the plant or in the office. You may recall that I had my ideas up there with my picture as well. I really worked at improving our supplier relationships and sharing with them what we'd learned. I was proud to have my picture up there. It was exciting."

"THE BOTTOM LINE EFFECT IS TO REDUCE COSTS AND CYCLE TIME WHILE IMPROVING QUALITY, SERVICE AND INDIVIDUAL INVOLVEMENT."

"Of course I do. But I thought we were doing all that with our brainstorming and quality improvement program. I kind of wrote it off as a motivational gimmick, I guess. But now I'd bet that's why SynergyCorp was so excited to help us. I'd also bet they have their pictures on the wall somewhere in their plan, too, don't they, Bill," Mitch asked in a rhetorical manner, not expecting an answer.

What Goes Around, Comes Around

"YES THEY DO. THE IDEAS THAT WERE IMPLEMENTED at your plant last Thursday and Friday were from some of their front line employees, not managers. That all began with a focus on developing our suppliers — their productivity and production capacity. They put in place Inspired Scorekeeping for Inspired Performance. That's what drove their innovation. But what it really did was increase their desire to serve their customers, not just deliver world-class products. You know, Mitch, 'what goes around comes around' is true. Last week you became the direct beneficiary of the focus we placed on developing them."

"They told me how grateful they were to you for the opportunity to help us out in our crisis situation. I remember just before we all went home late Friday evening Joseph asked if we could all have our picture taken together. I wonder if that picture is on their wall."

Bill didn't reply. After some silence Mitch countered with his concerns. "Bill, you know we have process improvement programs going right now. We have 'team management' already. Aren't we just saying much of the same things? Wouldn't we just be adding another program? I'm afraid they'll just view it as something new we're imposing on them. Another 'sheep dip' as I've heard some of our programs referred to. Last year we invested in fifty hours of training for each employee, and even though a lot of good came out of it, I don't feel it was nearly as successful as what I saw from SynergyCorp when they delivered those parts. What they really brought to us was their spirit."

Utilizing the Forces of Change to Build Trust

"MITCH, THERE'S AN INTERVENTION PROCESS WE'LL USE TO DEAL with everyone's past experience with previous improvement efforts. It's called Mastering the Senior Forces of Change. It establishes trust as the basis of every relationship. Trust must be at the core of every program. Without trust being there, and people knowing that you personally care about them and their ideas, this won't work. That is the process that we developed and used at the Plywood plant where every manager spent time building trust one person at a time until the shift to being aligned took place."

What People Want

"REMEMBER, PEOPLE WANT MOST OF ALL TO BE PART of something bigger than themselves, where their ideas truly make a difference — not where they're implementing a total quality program or some other process improvement concept that they've been sold by management. It must be theirs. I mean, you do know that we implemented all of your programs that we were asked to.

There's a huge difference," Bill said emphatically. "It is about ownership. Our people never owned 'your' programs."

"Just like the cowboy and the bridge," Mitch thought to himself.

Ownership and Personal Responsibility

"WITH OWNERSHIP, EACH INDIVIDUAL TAKES COMPLETE RESPONSIBILITY for their space, focusing on areas where they can implement improvements successfully. It only builds from the ground up. This is not top down. It comes from small improvements, from every employee being totally involved, all the time. I'm excited to show how and why it works."

"What the underlying structure of it is, you mean."

Everyone Wants to Change; They Just Don't Want to be Changed

"EXACTLY. IN THE WORK I'M NOW DOING, I FIND EVERYONE WANTS TO CHANGE. They want to increase satisfaction in their lives, make a contribution and do what it takes to realize their dreams. They just don't want to be changed. Because we lack self-awareness, we tend to try to change others, instead of finding balance within ourselves."

"Bill, when I was crossing the chasm at sunset last evening, I could no longer see the other side. I became rigid and frozen, right in the middle of the bridge. I was paralyzed. I heard the cowboy say (at least I think I did) to look within. When I did, I discovered an immediate calm in my mid-section, during what seemed like a terrifying moment. I felt centered when I focused within. Then I was able to move across the bridge with ease. Is that what you're describing?"

Crossing the Chasm Within Oneself

"ULTIMATELY, EVERYONE MUST CROSS HIS OR HER OWN CHASM. We must all go from being reactive and driven by our human nature, to fulfilling our purpose and serving others. Even though this needs to be initiated as part of the organization's developmental strategies, it is ultimately a choice that each individual must make. It's the only true choice a person can make once they accept personal responsibility and choose to control their own destiny. It's the choice to live a generative life.

"In the Indian way of describing it, some people are rigid like a stick and easily defeated or broken. They're too opinionated or dogmatic. They're blinded by their own point of view. Others are like a willow that bends whichever way the wind blows. They're too easily influenced. Both qualities exist within each person. Whichever one dominates our psyche leads to an imbalance. It's in finding a balance between the two that we discover satisfaction in each area of our life. It's also what allows us to maximize our contribution to others.

"In the council, we seek to disclose our imbalances and receive feedback from each other. That's where our strength as a council comes from. It's from trusting feedback. Once you have a purpose and dream to serve others, you see everyone serving you. That's the real purpose of the vision quest we must all go on....to learn to fulfill our purpose of serving others."

Once again, Mitch reflected on his own imbalances and recognized with relief that achieving his personal development areas could change all the results he was concerned about.

"Only from seeing these imbalances, which are unfortunately often hidden from us, can one choose a path that leads toward increased satisfaction. Then we can discover the power of focus, achieve clarity, and let go. Then we are able to cross the chasm of life and go from being self-serving to serving others; go from being managed to self-management.

"And Mitch," Bill said pointedly, "the cowboy, as you call him, was with me as you were crossing the chasm. Believe me, he said nothing. That was your own inner voice speaking to you on the bridge."

CHAPTER 14 *Creating the Future*

Bill made a simple drawing and said, "Mitch, there are those things about me that are known to you, but unknown to me. They are my blind spots. There are those things that I know about myself, but hide from you in how we work together. I did that a lot after you bought my company. Equally, there is a great deal that we go through life never knowing. These are often the very things that determine our personal destiny.

	Known to Me	*Unknown to Me*
Known to You	Shared Public	Hidden by Me
Unknown to You	Facade	Blind Spots

"Of course some are apparent and visible to everyone, both you and me. The difference is this: if the way I am conflicts with the way you are, we will not be able to become aligned and work together as well as we might have. So both our personal satisfaction and our relationship/team effectiveness are greatly impacted by our self-awareness. We will need to communicate in a manner that increases our shared areas and reduces our hidden areas. As we do that, our blind spots are revealed. Often they are the source of our greatest movement forward. I hope you will provide me with feedback and be open to mine as we work together.

When Aligned There is a Surge of Energy

"CLEARLY, ALL OF THIS REQUIRES A DEEP UNDERSTANDING OF ONESELF and of others. That's why the tribal council spends time in the sweat lodge before we meet. Sometimes they drum together for hours before addressing the vital issues of their nation. Then there's a surge of energy to accomplish truly remarkable things. I tell you Mitch, it's changed my life working with them in this manner. We're learning each other's differences. Now we're able to complement each other in very powerful ways. Until alignment is there, there can be no lasting change. When trust and alignment around our highest leverage points exists, the underlying structure is changed.

"Again, that's what the three insights are all about. It's all about energy... releasing it and establishing an underlying structure that will produce desirable results for the organization, for your organization.

"Well, I believe your horse is ready and your plane will be waiting for you. We both have much to do. After you've given all of this more thought, if you wish, we'll partner up and work together."

"Bill, I'm ready. The truth is we've already begun. The most important part of the work we have to do has already had a profound impact. I'd like you to map out the steps for us to take. I want to establish a Center for Inspired Performance at the very core and heart of our organization. We'll make the journey from reactive to generative together.

"THE MOST IMPORTANT PART OF THE WORK WE HAVE TO DO
HAS ALREADY HAD A PROFOUND IMPACT."

Nothing has Changed, Yet Nothing is the Same

"THANKS SO MUCH FOR INVITING ME HERE. I CAME NOT KNOWING WHAT TO EXPECT, but just wanting to get away from Atlanta and hopefully restore my energy. I really wanted to discover what SynergyCorp had discovered. Now I realize that I only knew what I didn't want any more. You have—indeed this whole experience has—released my energy and transformed my way of viewing everything. In a sense nothing has changed, yet everything is

180

different. I now know I'm committed to building a Gen
tion. There's no other real choice, is there?"

Bill remained silent. Gathering his notes, Mitch said
it just struck me that before I came out here my approa
all data gathering and analysis. You know," he said with a smile "the reports
I asked you to prepare and present? I was always focusing on systems
improvements and how to grow market share and cut costs. I'm sure you
heard me say it. 'All an organization is made up of are people, systems,
and processes. It's the bottom line that matters.' I was just spouting the
GT platitudes I had learned. I guess that's an example of sharing stuff
about myself that has been hidden from you. . . " Mitch continued without waiting for Bill's response.

"Well, it seems like we left 'seeing and feeling' out. I think we also left
people's hearts and spirits out of the process, too. We suppressed their energy
by making them wrong when they failed to implement the changes or achieve
the objectives which we set for them on our annual planning retreats. As
I'm speaking, I just realized that in another few weeks we're set to go off on
this year's retreat and do it to them all over again. I guess we'll have to bring
a bunch of drums and build a rather large sweat lodge." They both laughed
heartily. "Will you join us in doing that?" They laughed again.

Feeling the Pain

"SERIOUSLY," MITCH SAID, "WE CAN'T AFFORD ONE MORE CHANGE INITIATIVE that
doesn't address our failure to make fundamental choices and develop our
own pathway. It must be one based on principles. This time we have to
capture the hearts of our people by helping them to see the consequences
of how we've violated these principles. I know there's no other way. Just
as the brave had to face the investors who lost their money and feel the
depth of their pain, we need to feel the pain of our way of thinking as
well. We need to feel it at a deep emotional level. There's no alternative,"
he concluded resolutely.

"Bill, again, thanks so much. Well, I guess I better go..." Mitch said,
as he came over to Bill. And for the first time in a long time, since high
school sports, he hugged another man.

I am my Dream

MITCH CROSSED THE CHASM FEELING SO LIGHT. The burden he carried with him when he arrived was no longer there. Then he realized, "I am no longer who I thought I was—I'm not my self-image. I am my dream. That is what's actually different. It is who I am."

Energy swelled inside of him. He felt it deeply. It was at his very core. He paused in the middle of the bridge and did a complete 360-degree turn without holding on for dear life. Then it hit him. "I've let go of everything I was holding onto. In reality, it had hold of me. I didn't control my life, it did. So this is what freedom feels like," he exuded. "Incredible!"

The cowboy was waiting, and he smiled in greeting. They placed their feet in the stirrups, swung their legs over their mounts and began the trip down the mountain. As Mitch had always thought about him, the cowboy was truly a servant. Yet now he knew, deep within himself, that not only was he the brave in the story but he was restored as the designated leader of his nation. It was his destiny.

A Great Source of Strength

THE COWBOY PULLED UP HIS HORSE AT THE SPOT WHERE HE'D LEFT MITCH on the way up the trail. "Mr. Crandall," he said, "I have discovered a very few things in this lifetime. One is that all I can really do is make a fundamental choice to be 'true to myself.' Another is to 'seek to have health in all aspects of my life and relationships.' The third is that 'my freedom comes from being a servant to my people.' This knowledge, Mr. Crandall, and my personal relationship with God, is the source of my strength.

> "I AM NO LONGER WHO I THOUGHT I WAS—I'M NOT
> MY SELF-IMAGE. I AM MY DREAM."

The Parting

"I AM GOING TO LEAVE YOU HERE. You can follow the trail back to the airport. Just tie your horse to the hitching post where I met you. She will be cared for by a member of the tribe. Before moving on you might want to reflect on what you see. For the first time, he not only smiled but uttered a chuckle.

"One other thing, Mr. Crandall, I want you to have something." The cowboy reached into his saddlebag and handed Mitch a package. It was wrapped in cloth to protect it from the elements of the trail.

"Thanks for the honor of our meeting and letting me in some small way serve you, Mr. Crandall. We will meet again." The cowboy reached over and shook Mitch's hand, while at the same time making a gentle clique to his horse. He turned and was gone.

Breakdowns are the Source of Breakthroughs

GENTLY, MITCH UNWRAPPED THE PACKAGE. It contained a worn leather-bound book and another one that was new. He opened the worn one to discover a journal that the brave kept while on his vision quest. He knew that it contained the very heart and soul of the man who would now lead and restore his nation.

The first section was entitled *Breakdowns are the Source of Breakthroughs*

Another was entitled, *Reflections on Paradoxical Choices and Challenges*

The next was *Confronting and Slaying my Personal Dragons*

The final chapter was *Attaining Balance, Experiencing Rebirth and Discovering the Abundance of Life*

Once again Mitch was deeply moved, for he knew the cowboy had given him the key to his own personal vision quest. Somehow he also knew it contained the essence of what he required to develop the capability to lead his company through the challenges he would face in the days ahead and for his own sense of satisfaction and fulfillment. He also intuitively knew that he had been given a navigational guidance system for discovering his own leadership pathway. He had just scratched the surface of his personal journey, just as the brave had after he, too, thought he had it all. "Perhaps that's where it all starts," Mitch thought to himself, "with breakdowns.

"Well, I've a long flight ahead of me and I'll be able to reflect further on these writings. Perhaps I'll begin my own vision-quest journal." He opened the new book and, just as he suspected, all of the pages were blank.

Taking in the vista surrounding him one last time, it was not so much what he saw, Mitch realized, but rather how he felt. He felt connected, he felt alive. A deep reservoir of emotional energy was running through him. He was a part of nature, not apart from it. He was at peace with himself, and knew with a certainty that he was capable of contributing to others. And at that exact moment, he could see how everything around him was serving him.

He made a clicking sound and the horse responded, lurching forward with great energy.

As he rode up to the airstrip, Mitch could see his pilot emerge from the plane. Behind him, another person stepped out and waved. It was his youngest son, John.

APPENDIX *Excerpts from Chapter Seven:*
Bill and Mitch's Discussion and Charting
of Sales Effectiveness Over Time

"Think about it this way," Bill suggested, "You've been growing rapidly — so what has increased? Then what has decreased as each of these areas has increased? Note all of those things that happen that are unwanted. I'll quiz you on the quick fix or reactive behavior and see if we can conclude what the long-term consequence of your reactive behavior might be."

"Well, I would start with the increase in both the number of accounts and the complexity of each order. Our success has resulted in an increase in the number of accounts that each sales person has to manage. We were getting higher margins on custom work, so we really went after that. This has required more detailed specifications, of course. The amount of service time required on each account has increased dramatically. The complexity of each order and the number of changes from the client has also increased. Is this what you're looking for, Bill?"

"Yes. Now also consider, as each of these areas is increasing, what has decreased that has caused other things to increase down stream? That understanding is critical for this exercise. Then we will be able to take a deeper cut at causality and really dig into the source of recurring upset conditions. That's what we want to get to first with the little time we have today.

"So now we'll set up a simple x-y graph and chart each pattern of upset conditions. As you cover them, I'll categorize them either as what you would describe as a recurring event (RE), quick fix (QF), or long-term consequence (LTC).

"Over the past five years, say, what has been the increase in the number of orders? What about the complexity of orders? As a result of the increases in complexity and numbers of orders, what else has increased? What has decreased?"

Mitch was scribbling as fast as he could while Bill was talking.

"Let's exhaust this. Make sure we capture all of the upset conditions.

We're searching for any areas of upset that you experience on a daily, monthly or annual basis that affect all aspects of the business."

Charting Patterns of Behavior over Time

As he moved away from the flipchart, Bill said, "Mitch, why don't you chart events over time and I will categorize them as we go along?"

Hesitantly picking up a marker, Mitch began to fill in some areas. "Here's what goes on, Bill, but since you've already done this please help if I leave anything out."

"Believe me, Mitch, you'll get them all. You live with them day in and day out."

As Mitch listed each event, Bill labeled them with an RE. As they continued, he did the same with quick fixes, QF, and the long-term consequence, LTC.

At the top of the flip chart Bill wrote **Sales Effectiveness:**

Then he listed each pattern, as Mitch charted them. In each case, the charted patterns revealed gaps that clearly dramatized the impact the increase in orders and complexity had on productivity, costs, quality and forecast accuracy. Ultimately it could be seen how sales effectiveness actually declined due to a constant focus on increased sales, additional branches and new product lines — the very things they were doing to be more effective.

As they progressed in a rather iterative fashion (examining each pattern of recurring events and upset conditions) it looked somewhat like this:

[The recurring events **RE**] [The quick fixes **QF**] [The long-term consequence **LTC**]

1. **RE**: number of accounts that each salesperson manages increases; **QF**: less time spent on specifications and fewer visits to client site; **LTC**: inaccurate specifications, requiring more time on client site dealing with cost-of-quality issues.
2. **RE**: incomplete, inaccurate orders; **QF**: changes, rework; **LTC**: costs increased (projected margins on accounts' profitability dropped). Changes demanded more service, sales and operations people and increased production and engineering capacity to address them and

perform the rework.

3. **RE**: customer upset with quality; **QF**: give deductions & credits to customers; **LTC**: negative customer perception led to loss of business.

4. **RE**: production lead time decreases as deadline pressure increases; **QF**: pressure to ship without complete testing; **LTC**: more redos, changes, backorders, angry customers.

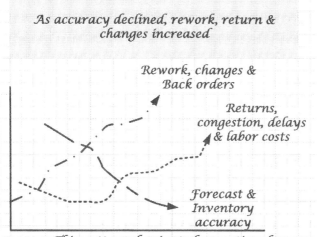

As accuracy declined, rework, return & changes increased

Rework, changes & Back orders

Returns, congestion, delays & labor costs

Forecast & Inventory accuracy

This pattern dominated operational productivity & sales effectiveness

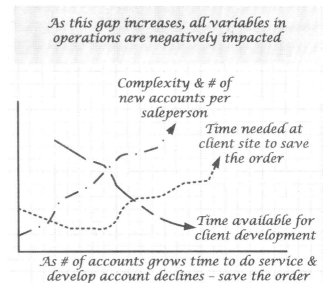

As this gap increases, all variables in operations are negatively impacted

Complexity & # of new accounts per saleperson

Time needed at client site to save the order

Time available for client development

As # of accounts grows time to do service & develop account declines – save the order behavior dominates sales

As Mitch dug deeper, it was clear that increased sales and complexity had an amplified impact, especially when it led to changes and even small amounts of rework, that originally were thought to be acceptable. It revealed:

1. **RE**: # of change orders and # of new products increased; **QF**: send senior engineers to client site; **LTC**: delays in other orders, which need to be engineered, now become rush orders. More small change orders resulted in loss of margins and lead time on existing orders. Everything seemed to cause more pressure.

2. **RE**: the salespersons lack of in-depth knowledge of complex orders; **QF**: give the customer more credits, deductions, and concessions; **LTC**: no confidence in new products; loss of competitive advantage.

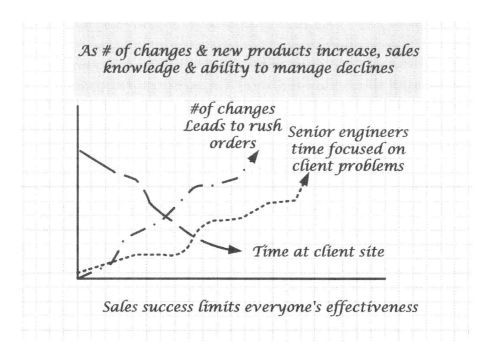

As # of changes & new products increase, sales knowledge & ability to manage declines

#of changes Leads to rush orders

Senior engineers time focused on client problems

Time at client site

Sales success limits everyone's effectiveness

Mitch could see how the increase in rush and change orders caused existing orders to be delayed, ultimately turning a higher and higher percentage of them into rush orders as well.

1. **RE**: rush orders; **QF**: change delivery schedules; **LTC**: all other orders delayed and rushed.

2. **RE**: rush changes on deliveries; **QF**: take short cuts on quality, etc.; **LTC**: loss of time, delivery delays, each order taking more time in the long run.

3. **RE**: equipment over-stressed and maintenance delayed; **QF**: fix it when it breaks down; **LTC**: equipment life reduced, operator productivity loss, poor attitude about equipment.

4. **RE**: back orders and late deliveries; **QF**: pay overtime; **LTC**: frustration, burnout, and turnover.

5. **RE**: customer demands and interruptions; **QF**: take resources from regular schedule; **LTC**: inventory errors, shortage of resources, overtime, and loss of productivity.

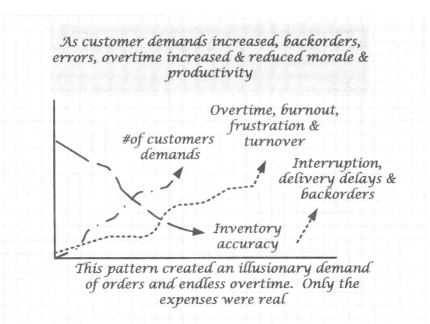

As customer demands increased, backorders, errors, overtime increased & reduced morale & productivity

#of customers demands

Overtime, burnout, frustration & turnover

Interruption, delivery delays & backorders

Inventory accuracy

This pattern created an illusionary demand of orders and endless overtime. Only the expenses were real

In a rather sudden burst of energy, Mitch shifted his focus to the impact of his top line approach: "increase the number of orders" at all costs. He revealed the impact this had on himself, his management team and the morale and turnover on the frontline. You could hear the pain in his voice as he acknowledged the impact it had on his people. When charted, it looked like this:

1. **RE**: stress, overtime, turnover of personnel; **QF**: quick hires to fill openings; **LTC**: loss of knowledge and experience in the workforce led to even more errors, pressure and turnover.
2. **RE**: new product complexity and backorders; **QF**: order more inventory; **LTC**: warehouse congestion, damage, equipment shortages, conflicts between departments.
3. **RE**: new product rollout (without training, capacity, or inventory to handle it); **QF**: the quick fix for the sales force was to not sell product; **LTC**: failure of rollout, loss of vendor and sales force trust; over-ordered stock is not sold, reducing warehouse space, productivity and increasing interest on money.

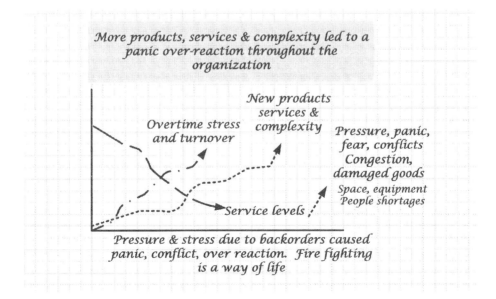

Then, with a good deal of chagrin, Mitch admitted, "We still stuck to our growth strategy of opening new branches to capture market share." As he charted this strategy, the impact was quite clear — as each branch had a time line to reach profitability. "We had a strategy of sending in a team of top sales people to drive the new business, even providing incentives to customers to change from their current supplier to us. Each change proved costly."

1. **RE:** expansion and new branches drain sales and experienced people from productive branches; **QF:** make quick sales by promising beyond capacity to deliver; **LTC:** one new branch effects all branches, margins decline, constant pressure to increase sales to make up for loss of experienced personnel and productivity.

2. **RE:** management pressure on sales volume and the fear of lost business; **QF:** give in to sales/client demands; **LTC:** no accountability and loss of margins.

3. **RE:** total profits continued to increase due to volume purchasing, rebates and increase in gross sales. **QF:** add more offices to drive the volume and meet investor expectations; **LTC:** margins continued to decline, the cost of arrogance went way up

4. **RE:** low unemployment, no experienced workforce; **QF:** hire without time to train; **LTC:** losing good workers and higher turnover of total work force.

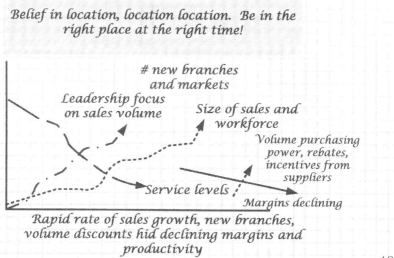

Belief in location, location location. Be in the right place at the right time!

new branches and markets

Leadership focus on sales volume

Size of sales and workforce

Volume purchasing power, rebates, incentives from suppliers

Service levels

Margins declining

Rapid rate of sales growth, new branches, volume discounts hid declining margins and productivity

"Now," Bill instructed, "couple all of these patterns with the other recurring events listed below. All of them have quick fixes and long term consequences. Notice how they multiply the cost and reinforce the effect of the above patterns on the organization."

1. **RE:** poor parts quality; **QF:** fix in the field; **LTC:** warranty charges, repair time and costs.
2. **RE:** manufacturing late on deliveries; **QF:** quit selling product; **C:** lose business.
3. **RE:** conflicts between operations & sales; **QF:** make promises; **LTC:** more quick fixes (see above).
4. **RE:** competitors hire away best people; **QF:** offer increase in pay to keep people; **LTC:** payroll costs increase for all employees.
5. **RE:** competitors' lower price; **QF:** we lower our price; **LTC:** create price war in some markets.

Feeling a bit overwhelmed, Mitch said, "I think we've captured most of the upset conditions that I'm aware of. These are most of the issues we've identified as our major problem-solving issues, anyway. And believe me, we have been working on them."

"Great. Now we're going to move to the third level of generative vision and examine the underlying structure that causes these patterns."

Causality and Mapping the Underlying Structure
Distinguishing between Organizational Behavior and Structure

Moving back to the flip chart, Bill began tearing off several of the worksheets and taping them to the wall. "The patterns we have charted are called **organizational behavior.** Behavior changes over time. It needs to be clearly distinguished from structure. **Structure** is how the organization is made. It's how all of the parts relate to each other. We'll map out the structure by using the patterns we've charted as our guide."

Causal Feedback Loops

"So the first thing we'll do is build the core, or foundational **causal feedback loop** of the organization. That is what we refer to as the underlying structure. Remember that I said we would use the three insights, a few principles and the laws of nature. This is where the laws of nature come into view. The basic law of nature is also a causal feedback loop. We'll build a similar causal feedback loop for your company.

The Core or Foundational Loop

"Now let's take a look at your foundational feedback loop. It's generally revealed by looking at your basic sales effort, order entry, engineering and design, and production delivery process. For instance, in the sales cycle you make numerous sales calls to clients, then they go through an evaluative process, a proposal is issued, they do their due diligence and place an order. You begin the data gathering for specifications, design and engineering. You order work done by suppliers and order the necessary parts, etc. Then you manufacture, produce, assemble and ship the product. An invoice follows and you get paid. Then you can increase your sales budget to grow your business, add more branches to expand your market share and the cycle begins all over again."

Moving back to the wall with the charts, Bill pointed out how this process tracks with the number of orders on the first chart they produced. He also noted how the number of orders increased and decreased — even though, if you were to average them — they would trend upward. "Some of them definitely came from acquisitions, such as buying my company in 1998."

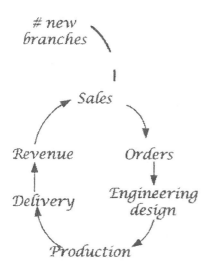

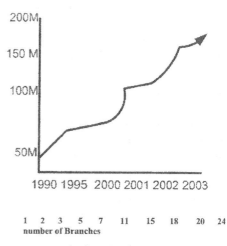

1	2	3	5	7	11	15	18	20	24

number of Branches

42	80	120	170	220	300	400	450	500	600

Number of Employees

"Yes, but that was part of the growth strategy." Mitch reacted, somewhat defensively.

"I know. Now let's look back at some of the charts to see what else increased and what decreased. When did the rate of increased orders actually start to decline within each of the companies you acquired as well as those in the parent company, Mitch? What kind of engineering and supplier problems increased?"

"Well, as we acquired each company, we'd pull our top managers out of their current roles (where things were going smoothly) and place them in the acquired company to help get them off the ground and beef up their sales. We wanted to immediately take advantage of the merger in all aspects of the business, including inserting our supplier agreements, national sales and service capabilities. Things like that.

"It worked like clockwork for about six months, and then we noticed problems starting to emerge everywhere. That's when we really became reactive, I believe," Mitch said reflectively. "We definitely added our engineering muscle to their sales efforts and captured the more customized, higher margin business. It was almost a slam-dunk for us until the capability within each of the new companies was strained and the demands put on our existing engineering capability exceeded our ability to respond. In most cases, the existing sales force just didn't have the sophistication for customized work. They tended to take orders as though they were still in catalog items or stock manufacturing. Some never did make the transition and we had to let them go. Then they went across the street and joined — or even became — our direct competitor."

Balancing Loops Determine your Rate of Growth

"Thanks, that's exactly the kind of analysis that allows us to develop a representative underlying structure. What happened as your growing secondary feedback loops began to develop? They're what really control your rate of growth. They're called Balancing Loops."

As Mitch continued talking, Bill started drawing feedback loops that represented the scenarios Mitch was describing. When he finished, they seemed to perfectly illustrate everything Mitch said he was going through.

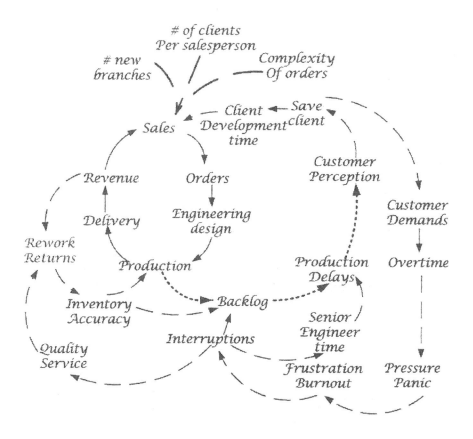

Look for Reservoir and Capacity Limitations

"MITCH, AT THIS POINT, IT WOULD BE GOOD TO EXPLORE AND UNDERSTAND THE significance of each variable seen in your underlying structure that we just mapped out. Each variable in these maps has a capacity limitation. They are like reservoirs. Think about having a bunch of bathtubs everywhere that can only hold or do so much. Capacity limitations both influence and are influenced by multiple forces. These forces include competencies (intellectual, interpersonal, reasoning, communication skills, leadership abilities, etc.) motivations, emotional maturity, attitudes and pressure. Things like that. They're even affected by the amount of experience each person has. It all adds up, and begins to amplify or exacerbate each of the patterns of upset conditions we chartered earlier. You can do this with the rest of your management team when you get them together."

Seeing the Past, Present and Future

"THIS IS AMAZING," MITCH SAID, ALMOST STARTLING HIMSELF. "IT'S LIKE being able TO see the entire past, present and future of the organization, all at one moment in time. It's like I'm seeing it from above, but grounded in it all at the same time. I felt like this in the sweat lodge when I was looking at and experiencing what seemed like my entire life."

"At the time these things are happening, it's very difficult to see, or even notice them. Because you tend to be in a reactive state anyway (and of course are pursuing your objectives at all costs to meet investor expectations) you do not even notice what you've been charting out here."

MITCH CRANDALL'S NOTES:

What you focus on determines your results

Structure causes behavior

The three insights

Energy is never created or destroyed, it can only be
    suppressed or released

Everything is connected; when you create the illusion of being
    separate, you become disconnected and lose your energy

The six powers are there to destroy the illusion of separateness

Vision is seeing over time, space and causality

What you see is a projection of what's inside yourself

Cause is invisible. It's based on principles and laws

All we can control is where we place our attention

When aligned, energy is released

Balance is your competitive advantage

Clarity is all defining

What goes around comes around

You can only let people in, not get them to change

Alignment happens naturally from knowing, seeing and feeling

When you change, your whole world changes

Cause is separated in time and space from effects

Gratitude is the source of all grace

Yesterdays solutions are the source of today's problems

Energy begins to flow only when you are connected. To be
    connected you must be on purpose and serving others
      You can only serve a person's dream / desire to contribute
Vision is seeing the past, present and future
    It's seeing over time, space and causality
Structure causes behavior; to change behavior,
    change the structure
Freedom comes only from knowing and telling the truth
All I can manage is where I place my attention and
    being responsible
What you see is a reflection of where you come from

AUTHOR'S NOTES

Going from being Reactive to Generative: Experiencing the Shift

Being generative first requires understanding a few simple principles and working with them as though they were essential to achieving your dream of flight, of making a difference in the lives of others, of realizing what you stand for, and of fulfilling your purpose on this earth.

To master flight and design/build a plane, even of the most simplistic design, requires an understanding of the principles of aeronautics. The same is true if you are going to transform the energy available from the flow of a river into electrical power that can light an entire community.

This is equally true when building an organization. Without this understanding you are flying blind. You will believe you are flying into the clouds and gaining altitude while you are actually crashing into the side of a mountain. Most destructive or counterproductive decisions are made thinking they will improve or make things better when in fact they are only reinforcing the cause and long-term making matters far worse.

Beware of Better Before Worse!!

The Purpose of Laws and Principles is to Act as a Compass and Guide You In:

- Placing your attention and constantly clarifying your focus
- Leveraging and maximizing the use of an organization's assets, including, energy, time, human resources, brand identity, and fixed assets
- Releasing the creative force of all people to become goal setters and goal achievers, with each person managing their own level and degree of contribution
- Constantly truing and using feedback processes for correction
- Committing to guiding principles
- Increasing productivity through increasing production capacity and aligning the organization around leverage points
- Consciously applying attention until you achieve the right amount movement and momentum (this movement is defined as mission-critical results)

- Momentum is attained when everyone is going beyond their best past performance on a daily basis
- Viewing current conditions through an understanding of the tools and principles of structural thinking

Principles are the heart of a generative organization. Use them as your compass to determine your direction.

Principles of Dynamic Systems

First there are principles that determine how the underlying structure causes behavior (or patterns over time). This is all based on:

1. What exists accumulates in the reservoirs of organizational bathtubs.
2. You cannot directly control what accumulates in these bathtubs or how someone uses their capabilities or resources. If they are in a reactive state they will often abandon their real capabilities and go for quick fixes.
3. It is difficult to connect cause and effect because they take place in different times and space. (So no one really has a clue as to what is going on.)
4. Pressures build (events) finally getting someone's attention and mobilizing other forces (often reactive ones) that make matters worse.
5. Other sudden changes are caused by out-of-phase patterns acting together, resulting in a perfect storm.
6. Capacity of a reservoir expands or limits growth rates.

Laws that Rule the Generative Context

(violate them and you are back in the reaction state)

1. The Law of Dominion

You have Dominion over all things

All of one's dominion is determined by being on purpose and by serving. The things you have dominion over are called The Executive Elements. They are:

1. Time; 2. Things; 3. Consciousness; 4. Energy; 5. Structure

In a reactive state, you give up dominion over these things. You sacrifice your birth right (who you are and all you can do) for a quick fix! In a reactive state it seems like you do not have enough time, lack needed resources, have only self-serving people; energy is depleted and there is a lack of workable structure.

Dominion is available only to the leader who masters the principles of service. When one does not lead by serving, these same elements will cause suffering, frustration, and recurring patterns of upset conditions.

2. The Law of Perception

You only see from where you look. The world is your screen and you are the projector. What you see is just a projection of what is going on inside of yourself. It is greatly distorted by your beliefs, perceptions and judgments. Your own perceptions are often misperceptions and tend to deceive your judgment. Often what you project is false and misleads you, causing reactive, self-serving human 'survival' behavior.

3. The Law of Giving

You only have what you give. When you try to get (out of deficit), get begets get. There is no abundance.

4. The Law of Essence

You have complete dominion over what you give and whom you serve. Your purpose is to serve others.

5. The Law of Focus

You can only control what you focus on.

What you focus on determines the results you produce. What you have control over is where you place your attention. Place your attention on making fundamental choices, living by principles and the laws of nature.

Balance determines your optimum growth strategy.

Balance and an optimum rate of growth are the two sides of the same coin. You cannot have one without the other.

Balance is your competitive advantage.

Balance determines your optimum growth strategy. . . it determines how well you grow your organization — not just in size, products, and services, but in quality, maturity, vitality, energy, productivity, and profitability.

Vision: The ability to see

Your organizational vision (or blindness) determines your effectiveness and ability to navigate when utilizing your guidance system.

Your consciousness and attention will be directed by your ability to see over time, space and causality.

What you see will determine whether you react to an event and try to problem — solve your way out of it, or see it as a moment (in a pattern) over time.

Discover and work with "cause," establish and align everyone around leverage points to grow your organization at an optimum rate.

The Guidance System

It takes a navigational guidance system to attain and maintain an optimum rate of growth. If the guidance system is not fully operational and closely monitored, any thing or community (operational, interpersonal, and financial) that is out of balance within an organization can contaminate its' core and control all activities, action and decisions.

Building your navigational guidance system:
- Begin by restoring your vision to see generatively (five levels).
- Make the fundamental choice to be generative.
- Always work with and respect the laws of nature.

Steps in Applying the Principles of Structural Design

1. Treat the underlying structure as you would a flight simulator. Act as if you were an aeronautical engineer designing a new airplane.
2. Identify where the current goals are established. Are they are in the reinforcing (core) loop? Most often they will be. Examine the emotional tension (or conflict) that is driving the accomplishment of the stated (or unstated) goal. What goal/s is/are stated negatively that result in things that should not happen?
3. What shift in your focus will bring about a structural change — that will

cause a definitive change in the system behavior? (Check undesirable patterns that you charted over time.)

4. Validate that you have identified the leverage points that will reverse the patterns. Are they located in a balancing loop/s that are responsible for the current conditions you have focused on reversing, and do they cause a shift in the dominate core loop results?

5. Beware of counter forces and compensating feedback that resists all system changes that are attempted. When you initiate changes that are systemic in nature, you will often cause disturbing noise everywhere.

6. A Fundamental Change in thinking is required for success. Change will lead to previously inexperienced or uncomfortable behavior. You will definitely be in the learning zone — not the comfort zone!

Discovering & Working with Leverage Points

To get to the cause, never look where the problem is — it is almost never in the same time or space as the effect.

Leverage points are almost always found in the balancing loop and generally will take the form of a thermostat setting. They tend to be quite subtle in nature. They should always address the question:

"What does it take to maintain balance and achieve optimum growth?"

1. Identify leverage points: Ask, "What will remove the source of upset conditions and limits to growth?"

2. Examine the underlying structure of the organization that you have mapped out and discover the true source of upset conditions (hint: look for the source or cause of any imbalance.)

3. Most leverage points tend to be developmental in nature and are based on becoming a competency-development organization.

Lessons Learned From a Reactive Organization

1. The harder you push, the less you get. The result is less for more.
2. The more things change, the more they stay the same.
3. Don't try to dig your way out of a hole.
4. Yesterday's Solutions often cause today's problems.
5. You can only see effects — cause is invisible.
6. The more you try to control things, the more out of control they become.
7. Where you look from determines what you see.
8. The cure may be worse than the disease.
9. Everything is working perfectly and has a purpose.
10. Everything is happening to teach you something.
11. All perception is mis-perception.
12. It is not possible to change others.
13. Cause and effect are separated in time and space.
14. Control does not exist in the reinforcing loop.
15. Certainty is not clarity.
16. All real growth is developmental.
17. We are in the core competency development business.
18. Your competition's greatest advantage is your complacency and arrogance.
19. Your organization is working perfectly, doing exactly what it was designed to do.
20. Being bottom-line focused often achieves the opposite result, in both the short term and the long term.